CRAFT AN Elegant Wedding

OTHER BOOKS AVAILABLE FROM CHILTON
Robbie Fanning, Series Editor

CRAFT AN
Elegant Wedding

NAOMI BAKER & TAMMY YOUNG

CHILTON BOOK COMPANY
RADNOR, PENNSYLVANIA

Designed by Anthony Jacobson

Manufactured in the United States of America

Library of Congress Cataloging in Publication Data
Baker, Naomi.
    Craft an elegant wedding / Naomi Baker and Tammy Young.
      p. cm. — (Creative machine arts series)
    Includes index.
    ISBN 0-8019-8575-7
    1. Weddings—Planning. I. Young, Tammy. II. Title.
    III. Series.
    HQ745.B35   1995   94-38728
    395'.22—dc20   CIP

        2 3 4 5 6 7 8 9 0   4 3 2 1 9 8 7 6 5

Contents

Contents

Foreword

Weddings are one of life's joyous celebrations. Or at least they can be, with savvy planning and a little creativity. Problem is, most of us are novices when it comes to getting married (thankfully so), or helping someone else—a daughter, son, or friend—get married.

By relying on *Craft an Elegant Wedding,* you're in for less stress and guesswork, and a healthier checkbook balance. I hate to admit it, but before I read the manuscript, I was ready to be critical. One of my first books was *Sew a Beautiful Wedding,* so I felt some ownership of the topic. I was pleasantly surprised and impressed by how comprehensive, accessible, and downright practical the information was, from scheduling and party planning, to trousseau sewing, gown selection and keepsake crafting.

What I like best is Naomi and Tammy's clever combination of hand-crafted and purchased projects. Plus, they intentionally break away from the sewing-purist syndrome, integrating fast (and professional) fusing, gluing, and serging techniques seen on the finest ready-to-wear.

Very few of you are going to make everything. There's simply not enough time. Ready-mades can be affordable and, yes, equally lovely alternatives. Naomi and Tammy effectively mix-and-match purchased items with time-conscious make-it-yourself projects and embellishments.

For instance: buy your gown, but make your veil. When I worked at a bridal shop to pay for college expenses, I made veils by the dozens, and often thought: "I wonder if these brides realize how easily these veils go together?" Well, thanks to these authors, hard-to-find veil measurements and how-tos (pages 86-88) are no longer the exclusive domain of bridal shop backrooms.

For ready referral, put this book by your bedside, or carry it with you. Review the timetables, check off the "must-do" lists and visualize the wedding setting. (Go ahead—write in the margins, and use favorite magazine clippings as bookmarks.)

Then have fun picking projects that are fun and fast to craft. Elegant embroidered pillow shams (page 35) Monogrammed bottle covers for the rehearsal dinner (page 57) Custom-fitted petticoats for the bride and attendants (page 89) There's a favor, gift, accent or accessory to suit every style and budget.

Enjoy this book—and all the preparations, celebrations, and remembrances that weddings are.

Gail Brown

Author of *Gail Brown's All-New Instant Interiors; Quick Napkin Creations; Creative Serging Illustrated; Innovative Serging; Innovative Sewing*

Preface

There must be a wedding in your future if you're reading this book. We want to wish you the very best. The occasion may be your own marriage or that of a daughter, future daughter-in-law, other close relative, or friend.

We've planned this book to be simple for everyone—even those not skilled in sewing and crafts. Most of the suggested project ideas take only minimal time and effort. Someone with more advanced skills can add extra handwork, detailing, or other crafted embellishments.

Wedding styles and traditions are so varied today that it's practically impossible to write a guidebook with specific rules, answers, and solutions for every situation. Instead, we've tried to give you tips, ideas, projects, and information that will help you create an event that is best suited to the couple getting married.

Chapters 1 and 2 are devoted to planning and organizing—probably the most crucial part of a successful wedding. They'll help you determine just what you want the wedding to be and get you started smoothly. Plus you'll make two projects (see pages 11 and 20) to help even the least-organized person keep track of all the details.

Then the fun begins! The remainder of the book has lots of creative ideas to inspire you and help you personalize the wedding. We've included numerous imaginative options and 30 easy step-by-step projects, many that can be made in minutes.

Chapters 3 and 4 give you lots of simple suggestions and charming projects for the trousseau and the prewedding festivities. You'll learn how to make romantic shower decorations that can be easily reused at the reception (instructions begin on page 46).

Chapter 5 assists you in finding the wedding dress of your dreams, whether you buy, rent, borrow, have it made, or make it yourself. Then Chapter 6 outlines all of the accessory options, including easy do-it-yourself ideas to get exactly what you're looking for, even on a tight budget. For example, you can save lots of money by making a glamorous veil in minutes (see page 87).

Look to Chapter 7 for recommendations and how-tos on outfitting the rest of the wedding party. The final two chapters help you save even more with quick decorating tips galore for the ceremony and reception and fun suggestions for creative remembrances of the special

occasion. Discover all of the options for using the wedding dress in the future, beginning on page 117.

Let *Craft an Elegant Wedding* help you personalize the entire event. In this eminently practical guide, we lead you through a wide range of inspiring choices and techniques so that you can plan the wedding that is best for you.

Also included are special money-saving tips throughout to help you decide where to conserve or even where you might choose to splurge. In the back of the book, you'll find easy instructions for making bows and rosettes, special tips for using a glue gun, and other ideas for easy embellishments.

We hope you'll use this book to inspire and assist you in crafting a very special and unique wedding!

Naomi Baker
Tammy Young

Acknowledgments

Special thanks to sewing and decorating expert Gail Brown who has always supported and inspired us in our writing projects. Her encouragement, professionalism, and past experience in this subject have contributed significantly to our book.

Thanks also to sewing pro and Chilton Sew Better Seminar instructor Patsy Shields for sharing her super-simple ribbon rosette technique (see page 126).

And what would one of our books be without all of our terrific support team: Chris Hansen--widely recognized illustrator, sympathetic sounding board, and good friend; Robbie Fanning—our series editor, mentor, and moral support; Kathy Conover—senior editor and the dynamo behind putting it all together; and all of the other Chilton team—Chris Kuppig, Jeanine LaBorne, Nancy Ellis, Susan Clarey, Jeff Day, and Tony Jacobson—who helped with the direction and format of this book.

In addition, we want to especially recognize and thank all those who have most recently contributed ideas and inspiration (because our own weddings seem like so long ago) and those who have given us so much support:

🎀 Naomi's son and daughter-in-law, Matt and Caitlin, who gave us a reason (and the pleasure) to test much of the advice in this book—they were married while it was in progress.

🎀 Naomi's sister Dianne and her nieces, Debra and Sharlyn, whose examples of patience and fun in planning a wedding were a great inspiration.

🎀 Naomi's husband, Red, and other children, Todd and Allison, who give her the encouragement and freedom to write her books, forbearing her late hours and the samples and fabrics she spreads all over the house.

🎀 Tammy's special friends who patiently keep in touch while she's "locked up" finishing a book

and then welcome her back to the world with open arms when she's done.

🎀 The many other friends and relatives we've assisted with weddings—designing dresses, sewing, altering, and helping with detailed planning. The experiences have given us the knowledge—and fond memories—to write this book.

Another big thank you to Ellie Schneider and C. M. Offray & Son, Inc. for their generous contribution of the fine-quality ribbons used in our testing and cover photography.

The following are registered trademark names used in this book: *Band-Aid, Jewel Glue, Liquid Beads, Plexi 400, Seams Great, Styrofoam, Ultrasuede, Velcro,* and *Victory Fabric Glue.*

CHAPTER ONE

Take Time to Plan

Careful planning will make any wedding the best it can be—a unique and memorable occasion. Your extra efforts early on ensure that all of the details over which you have control will run smoothly.

A wedding symbolizes two people coming together to share the rest of their lives and is usually a loving and joyous celebration involving family, friends, and long-standing traditions. There are no special rules you must follow. Observe personal and local traditions and individual taste to select a wedding style that makes you most comfortable. After all, this is likely the most important event in the lives of any couple.

Also take into consideration the wishes of those family members and friends who mean most to the wedding couple. This will be a special event for all of them as well. You can stretch the rules to add personal touches to the wedding; just use common sense and try to make courteous and thoughtful decisions.

Although the bride is usually the focal point of the wedding, her fiancé is an important part of the support system. The couple should consult early about all of the major wedding decisions, because a wedding can be a complicated event, as well as an emotional and exciting time. Today, many grooms are taking a larger role in the planning and organization of their weddings.

This simple guide is meant to help you make the necessary arrangements smoothly and to provide inspiration for creatively personalizing this very special affair. The better prepared you are during the months of planning and preparation ahead, the easier and more enjoyable they will be.

Sanity Saver

With all the possible variables, few weddings come off without a small glitch or two (like the adorable flower girl catching the chicken pox or one of the attendants losing her luggage on the flight there). These are things you can't avoid, so try to maintain a sense of humor, be flexible, and know that everything will work out in the end. This should be a happy, loving, and exhilarating occasion, so don't let the little things get to you.

Your First Big Decisions

Congratulations are in order! The most important decision has already been made—another happy couple is getting married. The very first thing the future bride and groom should do is inform both sets of parents, especially if they will be involved financially in any way. If the respective parents have not met, now would be a good time to arrange a get-together.

If the bride was not given an engagement ring during the proposal, the couple will usually schedule a time in the near future to select one together.

You might also want to have an engagement party or dinner to announce the good news (see Chapter 4).

The next major decisions are when to have the wedding, where to hold it, the approximate number of guests you'll invite, and what type of wedding to plan. The future bride and groom should decide together, often with the help of other involved family members or friends, the date and location of the wedding.

When a couple prefers a specific location (such as a local church or other popular facility), availability of the site can influence the exact date, so these two decisions must go hand in hand. Also be sure to set the date far enough in advance to allow for adequate planning. Other considerations in setting the date may include:

🐚 Season of the year, day of the week, and time of day

Budget Helper

Morning and afternoon weddings are usually less expensive than evening ones because of the food and the amount of formality involved. Saturday is the most popular wedding day and June and October are the most popular months. Discounts may be offered for other dates and times.

🐚 The convenience of the majority of your guests, especially those you want most to attend--work and school schedules, conflicts with other major events, enough advance notice

🐚 For an outdoor wedding, select a date when the weather is usually good

🐚 For a candlelight wedding, choose a season other than summer, unless you plan to begin the ceremony very late

Budget Helper

Get more value for your wedding dollars by scheduling at off-peak hours, days, and seasons, if possible.

The type of wedding the couple wants can affect both the date and location. Consider the type of wedding ceremony you prefer. Formal weddings are as popular as ever today for first marriages, but informal ceremonies also work well for many. The amount you can afford to spend will also be a consideration at this point.

Many brides today tend to be more mature, with a well-developed sense of style, and are no longer as bound by tradition as their mother's generation was. Thirty percent of today's weddings are second marriages. Plan the kind of wedding that suits the age, lifestyle, traditions, and social situation of the bride and groom.

When the couple is not certain of the type of wedding and reception they want, there are several steps they can take before making the final decisions:

🐚 Talk to both families about the wedding plans

🐚 Consult your clergyman (or clergymen) for counseling and wedding procedures specific to your religion(s)

🐚 If you are planning a traditional wedding, invest in a wedding etiquette guide for answers to difficult questions, such as who stands together in the receiving line

🌢 Visit local bridal fairs

🌢 Use your public library for books, periodicals, and cassette tapes of musical selections

In order to determine the size of the wedding, the bride and groom should also discuss the guest list. Although the list needn't be finalized at this point, a good estimate should be made to determine if the size of the chosen facility is appropriate. This is also a good time to discuss the number of attendants you'd like and to agree on colors for the wedding, as well as for the future home—many a man has cringed upon finding his new bedroom decorated in pink!

Choosing a Wedding Style

The type of wedding should reflect the tastes and styles of the couple and their families. Once this difficult decision is made, the other choices will become easier.

Consider both the traditions and formality of the wedding. Traditions will vary depending on family, location, age, and current trends. With a few religious exceptions, the fact that either the bride or groom has been married before should have no effect on the size or style of the other's first wedding (check with your clergyman).

When deciding on the style of the wedding, ask yourselves these questions:

🌢 Do we want a formal, semiformal, or informal ceremony? Generally, the more formal the wedding, the more expensive.

🌢 Should the ceremony be religious or civil? About three-fourths of today's weddings are religious ceremonies performed by a clergyman. The remainder are civil ceremonies conducted by a judge, justice of the peace, or other officiant—legal requirements vary from state to state. A civil ceremony usually requires the least amount of preparation but can be a solemn, dignified, and charming occasion. Interfaith weddings are often held in a neutral location with a civil ceremony.

🌢 Will we hold it inside or outdoors (often less decorating expense)? What kind of location? What time of day?

🌢 What type of reception will we have—sit-down dinner (most expensive), buffet, hors d'oeuvres (good for an afternoon reception), brunch, or cake and punch (least expensive)? Where will we hold it?

🌢 Do we want to add special touches to the wedding to make it more unique or personal?

Budget Helper

Don't be afraid to choose a less expensive wedding style that reflects your leisure-time hobbies or passionate interests—a wedding on horseback and a barbecue reception with casual clothes, for example.

What traditions do we want to keep in the wedding?

Use the following general guidelines to determine how formal a wedding you would like to have:

FORMAL—
* Long white dress
* Formal men's attire
* Held in a church
* Evening (most formal) or afternoon
* Flowers and decorations
* Several attendants
* Catered reception

* Soloist
* Organist or other musicians
* At least 100 guests
* Engraved or printed invitations

SEMIFORMAL—
* Street length or simple floor-length dress with a simple headpiece
* Dark suits or dinner jackets
* Any time of day
* Fewer than 100 guests
* Fewer attendants—perhaps only a maid of honor and best man
* Engraved or printed invitations

INFORMAL—
* Can be the most intimate, yet the most sophisticated
* Street clothes, suits for men (unless other attire is specified on the invitation)
* Two attendants
* Morning or afternoon—not evening
* No more than 50 guests, all of whom will stay for the reception
* Floral decorations
* May be no processional or recessional
* Handwritten or novelty invitations

Selecting the Site

Begin looking for a wedding site right away, especially if the date is near or you've chosen a popular time. Some places book a year in advance, especially during popular months. Before looking, you should have already considered the date, the type of wedding you want, and the location (in general, if not specifically) that you would prefer. You will also have some idea of the number of guests you will invite and the amount you have to spend. (Detailed budgeting will be discussed later in this chapter.)

If you have decided to have a religious ceremony, it can be held in a church or at almost any other site. Holding the wedding in the church will probably be less expensive, especially for members, who usually get first choice of dates.

When arranging a church ceremony, gather the following information:

🕊 Who is the contact person for the site?

🕊 What is the fee for the clergyman and when is it paid?

🕊 Does any equipment need to be rented? (Don't make assumptions.)

🕊 What are the charges for the organist, utilities, cleanup, and any other expenses? Is there a printed fee schedule?

🕊 Are there stipulations for the type of music, photography, and decorating?

🕊 Is premarital counseling required?

When booking a wedding site outside a church, call around because prices vary widely. Most charge by the hour. Be sure to ask if there are any restrictions (on the number of guests, for example) and allow time for decorating and dressing as well as for taking pictures and cleaning up afterward. If you choose an outdoor spot, have an alternative in case of rain.

Budget Helper

Also ask if another wedding will be near the time of yours. You may be able to share flowers and decorations.

For a wedding outside a church, whether it be a religious or civil ceremony, consider:

🕊 Hotel or restaurant

🕊 Large mansion or historic site

🕊 College, university, or community center

🕊 Private club, home, or garden

🕊 Public park, beach, or other scenic spot

🕊 Place where the couple first met

🕊 Place of mutual interest, such as a sports facility, on a boat, or even midair while skydiving

When choosing a nontraditional wedding site, ask yourself if it is easily accessible and has adequate parking. Will you have as much privacy as you want? Can the facility also handle the type of reception you want?

Budget Helper

It will be less expensive to hold the ceremony and reception at the same site, especially in a hotel, for example, which will have staff and supplies readily available.

If you will need separate locations for the wedding ceremony and the reception, be sure to book both before finalizing your plans.

Setting a Budget

Recently wedding industry sources estimated that a formal wedding in this country costs between $15,000 and $25,000, with an average of $18,000. The bridal business takes in $35 billion a year—it's big business! But you don't need to spend a fortune.

The success of your wedding does not depend on a limitless budget. Thoughtful planning and organization are your keys to success. You'll first want to consult with both families and decide who is willing and able to pay for the wedding or for specific parts of the expenses. Customs are changing and there is more flexibility now on who pays for what. Many couples are older and able to finance and organize most of their own wedding. The groom's parents may host the wedding or contribute toward it. The bride's family is no longer obligated to meet all of the wedding costs alone.

As a general guideline, custom has traditionally dictated the following wedding obligations:

BRIDE AND FAMILY—
- Invitations and announcements
- Flowers for the ceremony and reception
- Gifts for the bridal attendants
- Wedding dress and accessories
- Ceremony fees
- Photography
- Groom's ring
- Reception expenses, including food and wedding cake

GROOM AND FAMILY—
- Bride's engagement and wedding ring
- Groom's outfit
- Church fees
- Gifts for groom's attendants
- Flowers for the bridal party, including the bridal bouquet and attendants' bouquets and boutonnieres
- Bride's wedding gift
- Honeymoon
- (In some areas, champagne or liquor for the reception)

ATTENDANTS—
- Transportation to town for the wedding
- Their wedding clothes
- Wedding gift
- Bridal shower, girls' night out, bachelor party

In a more contemporary arrangement, the bride's family might pay for the ceremony and officiant, music for the ceremony, the reception, and the cake. The groom's family might pay for transportation, beverages and music for the reception, and photography. The bride and groom might pay for their clothes, the wedding flowers, and invitations.

When you are planning the wedding, you should have an idea of what everyone is willing to spend—including the bride and groom. Then don't be swayed! Taking out a loan is not a good way to start a marriage.

Budget Helper

At this early stage, the engaged couple should discuss their financial plans for the future, not just for the wedding. Especially when one or both have prior investments and financial obligations, a prenuptial agreement may be in order. If so, consult an attorney before the marriage.

Everyone involved in planning the wedding needs to be honest about the financial situation. Ask yourselves if you feel that the money you are budgeting will be well spent or if you would prefer to spend more on a honeymoon, down payment for a house, or other financial commitments. Your financial situation may be limited by another wedding in the family soon, college expenses, medical bills, or loss of a job, for example, so don't overcommit yourselves if you have only a limited amount to spend.

Your wedding can be special and exciting, whether it is simple or elaborate, if you use care and creativity in your planning (and they're free!):

◦ On all pertinent budget items, ask yourself whether to rent, buy, or borrow.

◦ Because much of your cost is labor, enlist the volunteer help of family members and friends instead of paying for the service. Recognize special talents and achievements, such as flower arranging, dressmaking, and photography. Just be sure you can trust the assigned person to deliver the quality you expect.

◦ Economize by scheduling the wedding at off-peak times.

Budget Helper

More weddings are being held on Friday nights and Sunday afternoons for better rates. Holiday weddings can be more expensive and take more advance planning because you're competing for caterers and sites with holiday parties.

◦ Shop for the wedding goods and services just as you would shop for any other major purchase. Look around, compare prices, decide exactly what you want, and recognize the difference between value and economy.

◦ Always talk about what you can afford rather than what you would like. Suppliers expect to negotiate. To get the most for your money, you may need to cut back without cutting out.

◦ Be careful of hidden or added costs such as gratuities, taxes, delivery charges, rental fees, and overtime expenses.

◦ Is there a cancellation policy? It's best to have one along with a deposit in case the wedding needs to be rescheduled or called off for any number of reasons.

Before you finalize your budget, determine your priorities and allocate the most money to those things that are the highest priorities for you. For example, if having the dress of your dreams is a high priority, you may need to spend less on the reception. Or if you want the best photographer available and lots of photos of the entire event, you may save money on the gown by making or renting one. If anything on your list is a very low priority, eliminate it or find a less expensive substitute.

Use the following percentages as a general guideline for planning the wedding and adjust according to local costs and your own priorities:

Item	With 100 Guests	With 200 Guests
Invitations and thank-you notes	5%	3%
Photography	10%	10%
Flowers	5%	5%
Clothing	20%	10%
Ceremony	10%	8%
Reception*	40%	50%
Wedding cake	3%	3%
Miscellaneous*	7%	11%

* Note that the reception costs and miscellaneous expenses increase with the number of guests. The other costs will be less proportionately.

After you have made the first big decisions and done some research in your local area (prices vary widely from region to region), set a realistic amount you will spend for every component of the wedding. The wedding site and style, number of guests, and food served will all be major factors. Food is often the biggest single expense.

Don't forget to budget for any miscellaneous personal expenses in addition to those you would normally have, such as extra long distance telephone calls, additional clothes for parties, dinners out when you're too tired to cook, extra food for guests, rental cars, hairdresser, manicurist, and gifts to each other from the bride and groom.

THE WEDDING BUDGET

	Estimated %	Estimated Cost	Actual Cost	Who Will Pay?
Invitations and thank-you notes				
Printing	_____	_____	_____	_____
Postage	_____	_____	_____	_____
Other	_____	_____	_____	_____
_____	_____	_____	_____	_____
_____	_____	_____	_____	_____
		Total	_____	
Photography				
Engagement photos	_____	_____	_____	_____
Formal wedding photos	_____	_____	_____	_____
Albums	_____	_____	_____	_____
Candid shots	_____	_____	_____	_____
Videotaping	_____	_____	_____	_____
Newspaper photos	_____	_____	_____	_____
Other	_____	_____	_____	_____
_____	_____	_____	_____	_____
_____	_____	_____	_____	_____
		Total	_____	
Flowers				
For the ceremony	_____	_____	_____	_____
For the reception	_____	_____	_____	_____
Bouquets, corsages, boutonnieres	_____	_____	_____	_____
		Total	_____	
Clothing				
Bride's dress	_____	_____	_____	_____
Headpiece and/or veil	_____	_____	_____	_____
Bride's accessories	_____	_____	_____	_____
Attendants' accessories	_____	_____	_____	_____
Groom's attire	_____	_____	_____	_____
Other	_____	_____	_____	_____
_____	_____	_____	_____	_____
_____	_____	_____	_____	_____
		Total	_____	

	Estimated %	Estimated Cost	Actual Cost	Who Will Pay?

Wedding Ceremony
- Church or other site
- Officiant
- Organist
- Musicians/soloist
- Decorations other than flowers
- Guest book (or at reception)
- Programs
- Other
- _____
- _____
- _____

Total

Reception

(varies from $5 to $125 per guest)
- Site rental
- All food (other than the cake)
- Beverages
- Furniture and food service rental (including plates and silverware)
- Labor
- Decorations
- Entertainment
- Printed napkins
- Favors
- Other
- _____
- _____
- _____

Total

Wedding Cake
- Cake knife
- Toasting glasses

Total

Honeymoon
- Transportation
- Accommodations
- Food
- Entertainment
- Tips
- Clothing, including a going-away outfit

	Estimated %	Estimated Cost	Actual Cost	Who Will Pay?
Other	⎯⎯	⎯⎯	⎯⎯	⎯⎯
_____	⎯⎯	⎯⎯	⎯⎯	⎯⎯
_____	⎯⎯	⎯⎯	⎯⎯	⎯⎯
		Total	⎯⎯	

Miscellaneous Items

	Estimated %	Estimated Cost	Actual Cost	Who Will Pay?
Marriage license	⎯⎯	⎯⎯	⎯⎯	⎯⎯
Blood tests (if required)	⎯⎯	⎯⎯	⎯⎯	⎯⎯
Limousine	⎯⎯	⎯⎯	⎯⎯	⎯⎯
Trousseau expenses	⎯⎯	⎯⎯	⎯⎯	⎯⎯
Other transportation	⎯⎯	⎯⎯	⎯⎯	⎯⎯
Rehearsal dinner	⎯⎯	⎯⎯	⎯⎯	⎯⎯
Gifts to attendants	⎯⎯	⎯⎯	⎯⎯	⎯⎯
Gifts to hosts and hostesses	⎯⎯	⎯⎯	⎯⎯	⎯⎯
Gifts to other participants	⎯⎯	⎯⎯	⎯⎯	⎯⎯
Personal expenses	⎯⎯	⎯⎯	⎯⎯	⎯⎯
Other	⎯⎯	⎯⎯	⎯⎯	⎯⎯
_____	⎯⎯	⎯⎯	⎯⎯	⎯⎯
_____	⎯⎯	⎯⎯	⎯⎯	⎯⎯
_____	⎯⎯	⎯⎯	⎯⎯	⎯⎯
		Total	⎯⎯	

Total Wedding Expense *(add all category totals)* ⎯⎯⎯⎯

THE WEDDING BUDGET

Getting Organized

Once the big decisions about the wedding have been made, it's time to get organized! If you have a computer, check out the software available for wedding planning. Or adapt your current programs for scheduling, budgeting, correspondence, maintaining the guest list, printing (invitations, programs, schedules), and even addressing envelopes.

If you don't use a computer, there are a number of planning books and organizers on the market at book and stationery stores, but you can quickly make one yourself, design it specifically for your own wedding, and save the expense.

Personalized Wedding Planner

One of our favorite organizers is a loose-leaf, three-ring binder with a decorated cover, tabs and pages for each section, and pocket inserts to hold any important papers and records. (Fig. 1-1)

Fig. 1-1

MATERIALS NEEDED

(All materials are available at well-stocked office-supply stores.)

Three-ring binder in the bride's favorite color (use a 1½" or 2" size for a simpler wedding or a 3" size for a more elaborate occasion)

At least 12 tab pages

Lined writing paper (in a favorite pastel color, if desired)

At least 8 clear, large-capacity, heavy-duty, top-loading sheet protectors

(Continued, next column)

One or two clear, press-on laminating sheets close to the size of the notebook cover

Clippings, cutouts, photos, swatches of fabric, ribbon, or lace, and any other mementos to decorate the covers

Tacky glue

HOW-TOS

1. Arrange a collage of the clippings and other mementos on the front and back covers of the notebook, keeping them in place with a light layer of tacky glue. Apply a laminating sheet over the top of both covers, pressing by hand from the center out to remove any air bubbles. (Trim any excess to fit the cover.)

2. Label the tabs "Calendar" (you'll complete this in Outlining the Countdown, following), "Budget," and one for each budgeted category ("Invitations & Thank-Yous," "Photography," "Flowers," and so forth), beginning on page 8.

3. Put your completed budget in that section and add sheets of writing paper behind every other section. Copy the budgeted categories and amounts on the first page of each section. As you plan the wed-

ding, you will keep track of all the information you need, such as dates, times, places, names, addresses, and phone numbers (tape business cards to the pages if you have them). All pertinent information should be readily available in the planner. (Fig. 1-2)

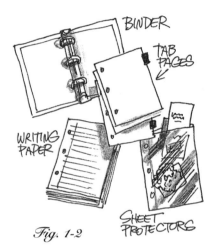

Fig. 1-2

4. Use the sheet protectors to store the contracts, receipts, price lists, brochures, pictures, swatches, clippings, correspondence copies, and any other material that you collect for reference or future mementos.

5. Add the Countdown from the next section and proceed to Chapter 2 to begin the detailed planning.

Outlining the Countdown

Don't use "too early" as an excuse to delay planning for the big day. The wedding takes only five minutes to an hour, but careful preparation can consume months. And with the careful preparation, you will avoid having to make hasty decisions, settling for your second or third choice on popular services and locations, and putting extra pressure on the bride and her family.

Be sure to allow enough time for the first steps in the planning process. Begin organizing a formal wedding at least six months in advance and an informal wedding at least three months before.

Earlier in this chapter, we discussed the first big decisions you will need to make. Check off the following items now to be sure that your initial plans are well under way:

❏ Discuss wedding plans with both families.

❏ Decide on the style of wedding you want and how formal it will be.

❏ Estimate how many guests you will invite.

❏ Determine the date and time of the wedding and schedule it with a clergyman, judge, or other officiant.

❏ Schedule a site for the ceremony (including the rehearsal) and reception. Get the exact site name(s) and address(es) for the invitations.

❏ Establish a budget for the wedding (see page 8).

If you have not completed any of the previous steps, add them at the beginning of the following list under "Calendar" in your planning book.

BEGIN NOW—

❏ Schedule time for the couple to meet with the clergyman, judge, or other officiant to determine any religious and legal requirements and to discuss the specifics of the ceremony.

❏ If the ceremony or reception will be in a home, plan any gardening, house decor, or house cleaning. Arrange for a tent or other major rentals if necessary.

❏ Begin the search for suppliers, including caterer(s), party rental service, florist, and photographer. Compare prices and engage services as soon as possible.

❏ Choose and ask attendants from among close friends and family (see Chapter 7). These may include maid or matron of honor, best man, bridesmaids, groomsmen (usually one for each bridesmaid), ushers (one for every fifty guests; groomsmen may also serve as ushers before the ceremony), flower girl, ring bearer, and junior attendants.

❏ Decide on a color scheme for the wedding. The colors will be coordinated through the brides-maids' dresses, groomsmen's tie and cummerbund, flowers, deco-rations, table linens, cake, and the centerpieces.

❏ Select the wedding dress. Will you purchase one (it may take months to arrive), rent one, make it yourself, or hire a dressmaker? Decide on the style of dress and veil you want. Begin shopping for the other accessories once you have made these decisions.

❏ Decide on the fabric and style for the bridesmaids' dresses. Will they be purchased, made by you, or made by a dressmaker? If they will be made, choose the fabric and pattern.

❏ Plan the menswear and arrange for a tuxedo rental shop.

❏ Coordinate the mothers' dress-es with the bridal and attendants' dresses.

❏ Shop for invitations and thank-you notes. Select the style you prefer.

❏ Begin a detailed guest list.

❏ Begin planning the reception.

❏ Plan the honeymoon. Make any reservations needed, includ-ing a nice room in town for the wedding night if you are not leav-ing until the next day. Apply for passports and visas, if necessary, and allow plenty of time (check with authorities locally).

❏ Plan the trousseau, including the going-away outfit and apparel for the honeymoon.

❏ Arrange for time off from work.

❑ Arrange any out-of-town transportation, if necessary, for the bride and groom or members of the wedding party.

❑ Reserve a block of rooms at a local hotel for out-of-town guests and wedding-party members.

❑ Make a calendar for the attendants and immediate families. Mark in the appropriate dates they'll need to know.

❑ Visit stores to compare for the bridal registry and select at least one

THREE MONTHS BEFORE—
❑ Finalize the guest list and set up a record-keeping system (see Chapter 2).

❑ Order invitations and thank-you notes. Proofread them carefully when they arrive.

❑ Begin addressing and stamping the envelopes.

❑ Finalize the reception plans and select the menu.

❑ Arrange for the rental of chairs, dishes, linens, and any other necessary items.

❑ Choose a photographer and go over plans for the wedding and reception. Take fabric swatches with the wedding colors.

❑ Confirm the florist (or florists). Order the floral pieces. Take fabric swatches with the wedding colors.

❑ Check with the bridesmaids regarding their dresses and shoes.

❑ Get measurements for the groom and attendants. Place an order with the tuxedo shop.

❑ Select the wedding rings (90 percent of men now choose to wear one).

❑ Make arrangements for the wedding cake. What kind do you prefer? Decide how it will be decorated. Do you want to use fresh flowers? A cake topper? Will it be made by a bakery or an experienced family member? (It's considered bad luck for the bride to make her own.)

❑ Confirm dates and arrangements with the officiant. Make the final decision on the ceremony and music. Ask when the fees should be paid.

❑ Decide on decorations (in addition to the flowers) for the ceremony.

❑ Confirm the ceremony and reception site(s).

TWO MONTHS BEFORE—
❑ Mail the wedding invitations. Record the acceptances if a card or an R.S.V.P. message was included.

❑ Record gifts as they are received and send thank-you notes immediately.

❑ Finalize or confirm reception arrangements, including the menu, cake, decorations, and favors.

❑ Ask specific family members or friends to help during the reception. Traditional positions include helping with gifts, helping with the guest book, cutting the cake, and hosting the reception.

❑ Purchase a cake topper, if you choose to have one.

❑ Purchase, borrow, or make any smaller items you'll need for the ceremony and reception, including a guest book and pen, a basket for the flower girl, a ring pillow, fake rings for the pillow, and a knife for cutting the cake.

❑ Tell shower hostesses where you are registered.

❑ Organize the wedding rehearsal and confirm the rehearsal dinner.

❑ Make appointments with a hair stylist and other beauty specialists. A manicure, pedicure, and makeup session are possibilities. Consider scheduling a hairstylist "practice run" with the headpiece.

❑ Make appointments for blood tests and any other necessary exams.

❑ Shop for gifts for the attendants, hosts, and hostesses.

❑ Schedule a gown fitting.

ONE MONTH BEFORE—
❑ Update the guest list by following up with any invited guests who haven't replied.
❑ Write thank-you notes for shower gifts. Also continue to write them immediately for wedding gifts.
❑ Double-check the reception details, including the caterer, menu, and cake. Make place cards if there will be assigned seating.
❑ Confirm that all clothes will be ready. Arrange for final fittings for both bridesmaids and the bride. If shoes will be dyed, arrange to have them all done at the same time.
❑ Confirm the time for the flowers to be delivered.

❑ Arrange for a wedding portrait, if desired.

❑ Prepare a newspaper announcement.

❑ Apply for the marriage license.

❑ Insure the wedding gifts.

❑ Decide where the bride, groom, and attendants will dress before the wedding.

❑ Make favors for the reception.

❑ Give or send a detailed schedule to all participants.

THREE WEEKS BEFORE—
❑ Finalize the rehearsal plans.

❑ Finalize and send invitations for the rehearsal dinner.

❑ Be sure all transportation has been planned.

❑ Make the decorations for the ceremony.

TWO WEEKS BEFORE—
❑ Confirm the number of wedding guests to the caterer.

❑ Double-check that all of the groom's attendants have been measured by the tuxedo shop or that the shop has been given their measurements.

❑ Break in the wedding shoes.

❑ Arrange for a bride's night out "with the girls" or a bridal luncheon.

❑ If the bride is changing her name and/or address, contact banks, credit card companies, social security, and employer.

ONE WEEK BEFORE—
❑ Make a followup confirmation with the florist, photographer, bakery, musicians, and officiant.

❑ Prepare a wedding program, if desired.

❑ Organize and pack all items you'll need for the ceremony and reception, such as the guest book and pen, the ring pillow, all decorations, candles, favors, cake knife, and special champagne glasses for the bride and groom.

❑ Pack a box of personal and fix-it items to circumvent any wedding-day mishaps. Include hairpins, hair spray, safety pins, needle and thread (with colors for the bride, bridesmaids, and mothers), small scissors, transparent tape, facial tissues, aspirin, antistatic spray, deodorant, brush, comb, makeup, and extra pantyhose.

❑ Open joint checking and savings accounts, if desired.

❑ Change the beneficiaries of life insurance policies and a will, if appropriate.

❑ Hold the rehearsal and rehearsal dinner.

ON THE WEDDING DAY—
❑ Attend to hairstyling and other beauty care. For a ceremony fairly early in the day, you might want to schedule part the day before, such as a manicure and pedicure.

❑ Allow for at least two hours to dress.

❑ Give the marriage license to the officiant, if you haven't already.

❑ Relax and enjoy!

AFTER THE WEDDING—
❑ Collect the bride's dress and accessories

❑ Collect the men's outfits and return them to the tuxedo shop.

❑ Take any wedding gifts home from the reception.

❑ Return any borrowed or rented items.

❑ Write thank-you notes to everyone who helped make the event a success and for any additional gifts.

In a Hurry?

A sudden job transfer, an unexpected opportunity, or simply a burning desire to hurry once the big decision has been made are just a few of the reasons why you may need to plan a wedding quickly. Not everyone has the luxury of enough time, but the results can be terrific anyway if you follow a few time-saving tips:

- Make arrangements for the clergyman or officiant immediately.

- Look for a site where you can hold both the ceremony and the reception.

- Select a less popular day and time for easy booking.

- Call for estimates instead of contacting suppliers in person.

- Simplify the details—a less complicated wedding can still be formal and quite sophisticated.

- Have fewer attendants. Have the bridesmaid's outfits in coordinating colors and like designs.

- Explain the time frame when shopping for a wedding dress.

- Delegate as much as possible and use your time for followup.

CHAPTER TWO
Getting Started

Now that you've made your major wedding decisions, prepared a budget, put together a calendar, and organized it all in your wedding planner notebook, it's time to get down to details.

At this point you may be feeling a bit overwhelmed, but don't worry! As you work through this chapter and the rest of the book, all the pieces will fall neatly into place.

Try to be realistic about what you can accomplish yourself in the time before the wedding. Analyze your strengths and weak-

Sanity Saver

Be flexible. If you realize you need to spend more on one part of the wedding, look for ways to cut back on others. If something you initially wanted isn't working out, brainstorm to come up with an alternative— it will probably be better!

nesses. Decide how much time you can realistically spend. And think about which aspects of the wedding you would most like to take on yourself.

Anything that will be a potential problem for you from a time, ability, or interest standpoint should be delegated. In most communities, there are competent wedding planners available, and don't overlook offers of help from your friends and family. If others are willing to pick up the printed invitations, help address invitations, or arrange transportation to the church, why not let them? This will allow you to take on the more important responsibilities and all you'll need to do is follow up to make sure each job is done.

Choosing a Wedding Consultant

The terms "wedding consultant," "bridal consultant," and "wedding coordinator" all describe a professional you can hire to help plan, organize, and see you through a wedding.

WHEN SHOULD YOU USE A CONSULTANT?—

• If you don't have the time or inclination to plan the wedding yourself.

• If the wedding will be out of town and the arrangements will be difficult to make.

• If you are not familiar with the community, local traditions, or preferred suppliers.

• If you tend to be disorganized and don't trust yourself to change at this point.

WHAT CAN A CONSULTANT DO FOR YOU?—

An experienced wedding consultant can take a great deal of the stress out of planning a wedding by checking on every detail, negotiating with suppliers, making some decisions and consulting you on others, and planning, supervising, and coordinating the entire event. A good consultant will not only save you time and pressure but also can save you money. She (or he) can help you budget wisely because she will know how to keep the prices down, who gives discounts, and who to trust to get each job done right. Remember, for most suppliers, yours will be a one-time job. But consultants will use a supplier again and again, so they will often try much harder to please her and continue getting her business-—then she can pass any savings on to you.

HOW DO YOU FIND A GOOD CONSULTANT?—

The type of wedding consultant we are discussing here is a free-lance professional who works for a fee. Don't confuse her with those consultants who work for department stores, florists, or other suppliers. They can be helpful if you are planning a wedding yourself and already have decided to use their employer's services, but they cannot help you coordinate the entire event.

Budget Helper

If you're having a simple church wedding, some churches do have a wedding coordinator who can help you with the on-site details for a lower fee than a wedding consultant.

The best way to find a good consultant is through friends and word-of-mouth referrals. When you interview a consultant, ask these questions:

What is your fee and how is it determined?—Some charge by the hour ($25 and up), some charge a percentage of the wedding budget (10 to 20 percent), and others charge a flat fee. Be sure to negotiate the fee in advance and adjust your budget, if necessary.

How much experience have you had?—Find out how many weddings she has done, and get names of past clients for reference. Ask what size weddings she has done and how long she has been working as a wedding consultant in the community.

Do you work with only certain suppliers or do you have a good rapport with several?—Ask if she receives a commission from some suppliers—be wary because that money will come right out of the price you pay. Stress that you are not willing to pay for commissions. Inquire which caterers, party supply houses, stationers, florists, musicians, and bakers she usually uses.

How much input will I have?—In most cases, this should be up to you, but it needs to be spelled out before hiring. Do you want her to confirm every detail with you before contracting? Will you sign the contracts or will she? Do you want to add personal touches? How does she react to the level of involvement you

think will make you most comfortable?

WHAT ARE THE OPTIONS WHEN HIRING A CONSULTANT?—

Your consultant can be as involved as you want her to be. You can hire her for the entire event or for a single task. She can help arrange all the details of the reception, ceremony, and the entire wedding, including gathering invitation and floral samples, overseeing the schedule, and even helping the bride dress.

Instead of hiring a consultant for the entire wedding, you can hire her for a single session, if that is all you will need. She can help you make a schedule, develop a budget, and plan the wedding. For a single fee, the session can take several hours and complement your own efforts. Or you can hire her to handle only the parts of the wedding that you, for whatever reason, feel you want to turn over to a professional.

The other option, of course, is to plan the wedding entirely on your own—many people have done it very capably and many more will do it in the future. The job will require lots of time—planning an average wedding today can take up to two hundred hours! If you have access to a computer, check out the compatible wedding planning software available. It can help you keep track of many of the details, such as guest lists (including names, addresses, and telephone numbers) for the wedding and other events, appointments and a work call-up schedule, and your own gift registry, gift receipts, and thank-you notes. Some software packages even have a programmed questionnaire for interviewing florists, caterers, and photographers that you can adapt to fit your needs.

How do you work with a consultant?—

Start by sitting down with her and discussing your budget, where you want to have the wedding and reception, and what you want her to do for you. To allow her to do a better job, discuss your lifestyle, your interests and hobbies, and the style of wedding you want. Tell her the colors you have selected, the size of the bridal party, and any other pertinent details and preferences. Then keep in touch with her on a regular basis as the wedding plans progress.

Finalizing the Guest List

Use tact and good sense when finalizing your invitation list. Consider the amount you have budgeted and keep the list under control. The costs will depend on the number of people you invite.

Ask both families to submit a list of friends, family, and associates they wish to attend and set a deadline for receiving the lists from them. The bride and groom should also prepare their own list or lists by that date. Compile the final list, compromising with the families' suggestions, and give a copy of the final list to each set of parents so they can familiarize themselves with the names.

You will probably have to make some difficult choices. Follow these general guidelines:

• Decide which adult relatives you should invite and select a cutoff point. Aunts and uncles? First cousins? Don't exclude anyone for past slights or petty reasons.

• Which friends will you invite? How close are you to them or how close to them have you been in the past?

• What other adults should you include? Personal friends or business associates of the parents? Neighbors? Past or present teachers? Fellow church members?

• Who should you invite from the bride's or groom's workplace? Their immediate bosses? Other management? Those with whom they work closely? Anyone at all?

• Should children be invited? Will you cut off the invitations by age and exclude younger children? Will you provide a babysitting service during the event?

Budget Helper

If the list is too large for your budget or the site, try to compromise. A large engagement party and a small wedding with immediate family and close friends might be appropriate. You might also choose a large wedding with no reception or a smaller, less expensive one.

In general one-quarter of those invited are unable to attend, so you can invite more than you expect to be there. Just be sure to call and check with those who fail to respond, if you haven't heard from them.

Keep an accurate guest list with names, complete addresses, and telephone numbers at home and work. Note the names of husband, wife, and children. List whose acquaintance they are if you're unfamiliar with the name. Leave the list in a handy place because you'll be updating it and referring to it continually for addressing the invitations (record when they were sent), indicating acceptances and regrets, checking on those who don't respond, recording specific gifts and thank-you notes (for showers as well as the wedding), recording those people who volunteer to help (or host a related event) and the thank you or gift you sent them, and recording who was included in each party or shower. Everyone who attends a party or shower should be invited to the wedding, but be sure that anyone isn't invited to so many events that it becomes a burden.

There are several ways to keep an accurate list. You can use a computer database program (be sure everyone using it knows how to access it), an extra section in your planning notebook, an address book with loose-leaf pages that can be added as needed, or a special card file.

Guest List Card File

Instead of putting your guest list in one place and keeping track of your gifts separately, use this handy organizer to keep all of the information at your fingertips. (Fig. 2-1)

Fig. 2-1

MATERIALS NEEDED

An attractive recipe or card file box

Index cards to fit the box

Alphabetical dividers the size of the cards

Foil in gold, silver, and/or the wedding colors (from a craft or hobby store)

Foil or jewel glue, such as Plaid's *Liquid Beads* or Jones Tone's *Plexi 400*

Sealer recommended by the manufacturer or generic spray varnish

---

HOW-TOS

1. Following the manufacturer's instructions, use the glue to draw a design and/or write on the box lid and sides.

2. Put the box in a dry, dust-free place until the glue is completely clear—this can take up to 24 hours.

3. Place the foil with the color side up (dull side down) over the glue and press gently but firmly. (Fig. 2-2) Then peel away the foil sheet. Press and lift, using different colors if desired, until all the glue is covered.

DRAW DESIGN

PRESS FOIL

Fig. 2-2   AND PEEL

4. Apply the sealer or spray varnish to protect against dust, wear, and soiling.

5. Place the index cards and dividers in the box and begin filling in all of the necessary information, using one card for each family and filing the cards in alphabetical order. Record each gift, the date received, what store it came from (in case you need to

make an exchange), and the date the thank-you note was sent. It's also a good idea to list the gifts by number on your cards with a corresponding number on the gift itself.

Budget Helper

When you receive a gift, make certain it is not damaged. If it is, contact the store (not the giver) for a replacement. Keep the gift in its original box and save all the tags and labels.

Getting Down to the Nitty Gritty

If you choose to forgo a wedding consultant, you'll be responsible for all of the wedding details, so the best place to begin is with your wedding planning notebook (see page ___). If you'll be using a consultant, it's still important to keep track of her progress in the notebook—you just won't be doing all of the work!

Your planning notebook will give you a sense of security if you keep all pertinent details in it. Whenever you hire anyone or enlist volunteer help, **record the person's name, address, and telephone number** in the appropriate section—even if that person has simply given you ideas—you may want to consult them again. This will also be a big help when sending thank-you notes.

In each section of your planning notebook, record the names, addresses, and telephone numbers of the suppliers you will be visiting. Tape the business card of the ones you select on the back of the tab pages. Keep notes as you progress.

Get recommendations for suppliers from friends and family, a consultant, your church, a bridal fair, or other suppliers. When interviewing suppliers yourself, look for those who you feel will provide the best service:

🌿 Are they people you will feel comfortable working with?

🌿 Do they seem understanding and flexible about what you want and are they willing to work with you?

🌿 Will they stay within your budget with no hidden costs?

🌿 Are you able to communicate well with them? Remember, you'll be seeing or calling them on a regular basis when you follow the calendar you made in Chapter 1.

Get a contract from each supplier you'll be using. Ask questions, be sure you understand all of the details, and make sure the details are spelled out in the contract. Carefully read the entire contract before signing and check that it includes the date, hours, fees, any other charges, a cancellation clause, and the exact ser-

vice the supplier will be performing. Put down as small a deposit as possible, and never pay in full until the service has been completed to your specifications.

Budget Helper

Even if you've never planned an event like this, stand firm when working with the suppliers. When you're undecided about what you want, stay calm and don't let yourself be railroaded into something you'd rather not have—that can be expensive! Instead, take time to think it over before deciding. Get back to them later, if you're unsure.

Invitations and thank-you notes

Order your invitations just as soon as you have made your first big decisions (see Chapter 1) so that you will have plenty of time to address them. Order at least two months in advance—three months is preferable, in case an error is made in the printing.

Formal invitations are usually printed by large national companies who give catalogs to stationery stores, department stores, jewelry stores, printers, and churches (may be offered as a fund raiser). Mail order can be risky unless it's guaranteed, because you will pay for any mistakes.

When you interview each potential supplier, look at their samples for the typeface, paper stock (usually either white or off-white), and design that you prefer. Look at examples of engraving (the most expensive and formal), thermography (much less expensive but can be formal), and printing. Check the exact cost for each component you plan to order and ask if there is a price break after a certain amount. Also ask how much deposit is required (the average is 50 percent), how soon the order will arrive, who is responsible for any mistakes, and what are the terms if the order is canceled. If you are interested, you should also check whether they offer thank-you notes, printing or embossing of the return address on the envelopes, and recycled paper, as well as folding, stuffing, addressing, and mailing services.

Before you place your order, complete the following checklist:

❏ Our guest list is completed. We have decided who will be invited to the wedding only, to the reception only, or to both.

❏ We will send out ___ (how many?) invitations. Order one per family and an extra 25 or 30 in case you decide to invite a few more guests later and for remembrances for the immediate families.

❏ How formal will the wedding be and what type of invitation will reflect the chosen style? Do we know the typeface and paper stock we prefer? Will we use

engraving, thermography, printing, calligraphy, or handwriting? Do we want to design our own and add a personal touch? If so, exactly what do we want? (A handwritten invitation by the bride or her family can serve very well for a small, informal wedding. Read on for a number of creative options.)

❏ What is the exact wording we want on the invitation? Check an etiquette book for the proper wording for your circumstances—not all suppliers will know. (Also check for the proper form for addressing.) Confirm the date, time, and place of the wedding and reception and double check all spelling and addresses to be included in the printing. Does the invitation need to be bilingual?

❏ Will we have the return address printed or embossed on the envelopes? Order extra in case of addressing errors. If you won't have the envelopes printed, you can take them home earlier to begin addressing them.

❏ In addition to the invitations, do we want to include an inner envelope, reception cards (giving the location and time), response cards (telling whether the guests will be attending), response card envelopes (stamped and self-addressed, usually to the bride's parents), envelope linings or tissues (in a wedding color?), at-home cards, a printed or photo-copied map to help guests find the ceremony or reception?

Budget Helper

To save money, don't order all of the possible enclosures. For example, by printing the reception details on the invitation, you can save as much as 16 percent on your stationery bill. If the envelope is oversized, the postage could be more. Also ask the stationer to weigh all the pieces you have selected to mail with the invitation. How much postage will be required? Can you save by leaving out one item?

❑ Will we order thank-you notes with the bride's and groom's names printed on the front or will we make our own?

❑ Will we send announcement cards to anyone not invited? (This is most often done when the wedding is small or private. A regular invitation should be sent to anyone you want to attend, even if you know they will be unable to come.) How will we word the card? ("Have the pleasure to announce" is usually substituted for "request the 'honour' of your presence"or "request the pleasure of your company.")

❑ How much have we budgeted for all the wedding stationery? You might have to compromise by making your own invitations or thank-you notes.

Check with your post office to see if it has special commemorative stamps you would like to use. Purchase enough for first-class mail for your invitation, response card envelopes, and thank-you notes. When your invitations arrive, check them carefully for errors. Then stuff the addressed envelopes and mail them all at once. (Check an etiquette book or your stationer for the correct stuffing procedure for the pieces you have selected.)

Either the bride or groom should write a thank-you note as soon as each gift is received. (It's more modern, but not mandatory, for the groom to write those to his friends, family members, and acquaintances.) Thank-you notes should always be handwritten and personal, including recognition of the specific gift and how it will be used (especially money), saying thank you, and mentioning the spouse's name and his or her appreciation.

If you choose to design more creative invitations or thank-you notes, you can save money and also personalize the event. The invitation should complement the theme and formality of your wedding. Consider some of these ideas:

🕮 Use an unusual paper—handmade, scented, recycled, colored in the wedding colors, parchment printed with colored ink. Select envelopes to coordinate or match.

🕮 Design and print the invitations by computer—use calligraphy or a special font, add a picture of the bride and groom, select a favorite verse or write an original.

🕮 Add your own special artwork—a lace collage, rubber stamps and embossing powder, silk screening.

🕮 Press and glue dried flowers, leaves, or butterflies to the invitation.

🕮 Enclose a surprise in the envelope—paper or dried rose petals, an origami flower, ribbons, confetti. (But have a heart! Glitter can make too much of a mess.)

Photography

Prepare a specific list of all the pictures you would like to have taken, the types of shots, the persons to include, and the times you would like the photographs taken. Compare fees for everything, including formal portraits, personal and parents' albums, and all of the photos you would like to receive. Also consider these pointers:

🕮 Don't depend on family members if they aren't experienced photographers.

🍃 Ask the clergyman about the policy on picture taking during the ceremony.

🍃 An experienced photographer will always be in the right place at the right time. Ask whether he or she will use additional lighting, bring extra cameras, and allow other photography.

🍃 Ask for candid photos with human interest, too. Either give disposable cameras to several guests or have one person assigned to make suggestions to the photographer.

🍃 Don't limit yourself to the photographer's packages.

Budget Helper

You should get all the proofs from the photographer, so check before signing the contract. If you want to buy the originals for lower-cost duplication, be sure the price is stated in the contract.

Check with professional videographers or an experienced friend (hired or enlisted) if you want to videotape the event. This is a popular way to record a wedding and can be lots of fun at the reception, asking guests for comments and good wishes for the bride and groom. Be sure to have extra batteries and tapes on hand.

Flowers

It's hard to imagine a wedding without at least some flowers—they help lift the event out of the ordinary and make it a special fairy-tale-like day. Unfortunately, if you aren't careful, flowers can also be a large part of your wedding expense. Envision exactly what kinds and how many flower arrangements, bouquets, corsages, and boutonnieres you would like—this is a great place to show your creativity. Then decide how much of the work you will do yourself, have friends or relatives do, or hire professionals to do. See Chapter 8 for more detailed suggestions.

Flowers for a formal wedding might include:

🍃 A bridal bouquet—a cascade (if she's tall enough not to be overwhelmed by it), a rounded nosegay, a more casual spray, a wrist corsage or arm arrangement, a corsage (for a less formal wedding), flowers attached to a

CASCADE

SPRAY

NOSEGAY

SINGLE BLOSSOM

WRIST OR ARM ARRANGEMENT

prayer book or other special object, or even a single long-stemmed blossom. These are traditionally white or mostly white with some filler.

🍃 Bridal headpiece

🍃 Attendants' bouquets or corsages

🍃 Mothers' and grandmothers' corsages

🍃 Boutonnieres for the groomsmen, ushers, fathers, and grandfathers

🍃 Corsages or boutonnieres for others helping at the wedding

🍃 Altar arrangements

🍃 Flower girl basket

🍃 Other arrangements for the wedding site

🍃 Arrangements and/or garlands for the reception

🍃 Corsages or boutonnieres for those helping at the reception—punch and cake servers, guest book attendants, host and hostess, and any others

🍃 Rehearsal dinner centerpiece and corsages

🍃 Wedding cake decorations

As you call on potential suppliers, take samples of your wedding colors along, tell them the style you've selected for the wedding, and if you have a special theme. Listen to their suggestions and check prices for everything you want. Ask about delivery and the availability of specific flowers during the season (you may need to substitute). Also check out ribbon, silk flowers as well as real ones for some of the arrangements (especially during midwinter in colder climates), and the types of bouquets and arrangements available. When you sign a contract, be sure that the freshness of the flowers is guaranteed.

Budget Helper

Even if the groom will be paying for the bridal bouquet, boutonnieres, mothers' corsages, and any flowers for the rehearsal dinner (it's a tradition, but not always followed today), purchase all of the flowers together in order to get the best price. Then everything will be coordinated, too.

Because it's important to stay within your budget, you may have to cut costs in this area by doing some of the work yourself, enlisting the help of friends and relatives, and renting or borrowing part of what you'll need. Use blossoms and greenery from your yard or from neighbors, friends, and relatives. Rent or borrow vases, baskets, other props, potted plants, and even large arrangements.

"To personalize flower arrangements, take your favorite vases (or those of a relative?) to the florist. You'll love the unique looks created, and the vases will remain as a memento of the events. To avoid loss during the wedding and reception chaos, identify the owner of each vase by writing on tape fixed to the underside."

Gail Brown
Gail Brown's All-New
Instant Interiors

If you will be doing all or part of the flowers yourself, check out a good book on floral arrangement from the library. Check on purchasing flowers from a wholesale supplier. Visit a floral supply store for ribbon, floral wire and tape, silk or dried flowers to fill in, and other floral accessories. Look at their floor samples for ideas. Ask for suggestions or a demonstration on how to tie attractive bows or how to make any of your arrangements, bouquets, or corsages. This can be lots of fun if you have the time and interest for it. See Chapter 8 for some creative ideas.

Clothing

In the clothing section of your planning notebook, you can list the names, sizes, and measurements of each person in the wedding party. Detail each item of clothing they will need. Include pictures or pattern sketches, fabric swatches, and any other pertinent details.

Include the store, address, and telephone number where you saw something that inspired you or where you purchased specific items. Include a brochure from the tuxedo rental shop. List all prices and actual costs. Even if you won't be paying some of these costs yourself, someone must act as the coordinator so that everything goes smoothly in the end.

See Chapters 5 and 6 for a wide range of options when outfitting the bride. Chapter 7 gives you more creative ideas for coordinating the other members of the wedding party.

The wedding ceremony

In Chapter 1, we discussed selecting and scheduling the wedding site and arranging for the officiant. Add all of those details to this section of your planning notebook. What time can you get in and when must you leave? Is there a changing room for the bridal party? Will you need special personnel to help with sound or lights? Is there adequate parking? Should you use a valet parking service? Is there a place to hang coats if the weather dictates?

List all the pertinent information about the entire wedding party. Record any decorations you will use in addition to flowers, such as pew markers or candelabra, and where you will get them. What other small items will you need? A ring bearer's pillow? A kneeling bench or cushion? Will you have programs printed listing all participants and the progression of the ceremony? Will you give out small packets of birdseed to throw? (Rice can be dangerous for any birds who eat it.) Will you need a pen and guest book or wait for the reception?

Keep track of all the music you will play at the ceremony. List the information about the organist, soloist, and any other musical participant. Record the fee for each one. List the songs to be performed. Will you need to use the site's sound system or rent one? What is the fee? Do you need to furnish sheet music?

What other participants will you include in the ceremony? This is a good way to recognize those people who are most special to you. Some weddings have a junior bridesmaid or candle lighters. Others could read a selection during the ceremony,

pass out programs at the doors, coordinate and pin on flowers, help the bride and her attendants dress, or arrange the bride's train before she goes down the aisle. Keep track of each helper. Will you show them your appreciation with corsages and boutonnieres or a gift? Don't forget to send thank-you notes.

The reception

If the reception will be held at a separate site, you will need to go through several of the same planning questions as you did for the ceremony. What is the exact name and location of the site? Record the information about the contact person. Does it have enough electricity and a fully equipped kitchen? What is the rental fee? When can you get in and when must you leave? Can you do your own decorating? Will you need additional parking? Valets? Is there a place for hanging coats? Who else will you need to hire? Waiters? Bartenders? Are there liquor regulations?

Will you hire musicians or a disk jockey and what are their fees? List their contact information. Will you need a sound system? What type of music will they play? Any special songs?

What other helpers will you enlist? List all the information about anyone you ask to serve cake, ladle punch, attend the guest book, or help with gifts. If there is a host and hostess for the event, detail that too.

The largest job at the reception will be preparing the food. This often takes a great deal of organization. If you're fortunate enough to have a large group of helpful volunteers to bring dishes or do the cooking, the bride's family or someone else close to her may choose to take on the task. Many people, however, want to simply relax and enjoy this special time, so hiring a caterer is a common practice.

When selecting a caterer, look for experience and someone who helps you feel confident. When a facility (such as a hotel) has a caterer, you can often save by using theirs, but you may also choose to bring someone in from the outside. Most good caterers have organized and attended more wedding celebrations than everyone except a clergyman, so they can give you excellent advice on what works and what doesn't.

🌸 Ask lots of questions and be sure you understand the services offered.

🌸 How much will they charge and how is the charge determined? The charge is often per person, so you'll need an accurate count in advance of the number attending.

🌸 How many guests can they accommodate?

🌸 Do the prices vary with the time of day or the day of the week?

🌸 Exactly what will the caterer provide for the fee you are paying? What costs extra?

- What are the menu choices?

- Set the gratuity in advance.

- What size are the tables? How will they cover and decorate them? Will they use your wedding colors? Can you add decorations?

- When will they be there to set up? Who will supervise? When will the food service begin? Will they be cleaned up and out by the designated time? What is the fee for servers?

- Can they recommend other suppliers you might want to use?

Also list any other incidentals you will need to buy, rent, or borrow. Will you have favors? Who will prepare them and who will give them out? Will you have napkins printed? Do you want special champagne glasses and a silver cake server? Will you decorate them with ribbons and/or flowers? Refer to Chapter 8 for some creative suggestions on setting the scene.

The wedding cake

An elaborate wedding cake has long been part of the established wedding tradition. It pays to shop around for bakers because prices can vary widely. Some experienced cake makers work out of their home and usually charge less. Even the bakery section at some large supermarkets will make a lovely wedding cake for a good price. See page 112 for more detailed suggestions.

Before placing your order, decide what you want the cake to look like.

- How large and how many layers? Do you have a photo of one you really like?

- What type, flavor, and icing do you prefer?

- Take swatches of your colors if you want colored cake decorations to coordinate.

- Do you want to have a decorative topper on the cake? Will you give it to the baker or use one they supply?

- Will the cake be decorated with flowers, ribbons, or other ornaments? Who should order them? When will they be put on and by whom?

Budget Helper

Save money on the wedding cake by using a large decorated Styrofoam cake you either make or rent, then serve the guests from less expensive sheet cakes. Or order a smaller wedding cake and serve the rest from sheet cakes.

A special honeymoon

The details of the honeymoon need to be planned as carefully as those of the wedding. Any tickets and accommodations need to be handled well in advance. Other transportation details should be worked out. Clothing and other personal items need to be planned and packed. Will traveler's checks, passports, or any special gear be needed? Are there any arrangements you should make at home for the time you'll be gone?

Miscellaneous details

This section in your budget and your planning notebook covers all those extra things that go along with the wedding and will take some attention.

The bride and groom will usually need to have blood tests and then get a marriage license. What transportation do you need to arrange to and from the ceremony and reception? Will you hire a limousine? What gifts will you buy for your attendants, hosts, hostesses, and other participants? Will you need to plan accommodations, food, or transportation for out-of-town guests?

Record all the details for the rehearsal dinner if you are involved in planning it. Traditionally the groom's family organizes and pays for this event, but that is not always the case today, especially if they are from out of town.

Will you need new clothes for the prewedding celebrations?

What trousseau items do you want to gather or make prior to the wedding? Where will you live when you return from the honeymoon? Is your new home stocked and in move-in condition? Carefully go over all the details that pertain to your situation so that this will be a smooth transition into married life.

Registering with Local Stores

Many different types of stores and businesses—even mail-order catalogs—offer a bridal registry. A registry allows the couple to make a wish list for establishing their new home, detailing exactly what they would like to receive. Although few couples get everything on their list, it is very helpful in allowing them to receive things they will like and use.

Be sure to register early. It not only helps the couple, but it also makes it easier and more convenient for wedding, shower, and party guests to decide on gifts. Follow these suggestions:

🖐 Take time to consider carefully what type of lifestyle you will have in the future before you register. What will you need to coordinate with what you already have and like?

🖐 Look through magazines and go shopping to decide what styles and items you really like.

🖐 Think about the colors you want to use in your new home.

🖐 Before registering, know the standard size or specific dimensions of everything you want.

For example, what sizes are your beds, pillows, and tables? Are your tables round, square, or oblong, and, if expandable, what is that size?

🖐 Choose specific items of fine china, crystal, silver flatware, casual dinnerware, glassware, everyday flatware, table linens, cookware, cutlery, small appliances, and kitchenware. Also list any other items you really want, including furniture and decorative home accessories, bed and bath products, electronic or other home equipment, luggage, and stationery.

🖐 For each item you list, include the brand, color, design, and the number needed.

Budget Helper

Because you will rarely get every piece of the china, crystal, and silver you select, decide whether you want to spend your money filling in the sets or if you anticipate receiving the fill-in pieces as gifts on future occasions. It isn't necessary to register for every item or for every type of item. If you lead a very casual lifestyle and don't envision ever having formal dinners, you may want to get good everyday items only.

🖐 If you already have many of the usual wedding gift items (common with older couples or second marriages), choose some less traditional registry items. Register at a record store, computer store, bookstore, or garden shop. Consider services, lessons, sporting goods, business needs, or gourmet items.

🖐 Many stores have helpful in-store consultants and specific checklists to make your decisions easier, so do take advantage of them.

Register at more than one store, but don't register for the same items or you may receive duplicates. Decide all of the things you want, coordinating the colors, and divide up your list. Try to register with stores that accommodate both your own preferences and the convenience of your guests.

Select a range of prices at each store where you are registered. Include low-cost items for showers and those on a fixed budget, moderately priced suggestions,

and more expensive things for those who may want to pool funds.

When you register, put the list under both the bride's and groom's name and include the wedding date. As purchases are made, the list will be updated—now usually by computer. In fact, most department store chains can coordinate the purchases made at all of their branches.

Announce the registries before showers and parties or by word of

mouth. (Never include this information with the wedding invitation.)

Contact each registry every few weeks to double-check what you've received with their records. You can also add to the list if you forgot something or find new seasonal items the store has added that you would like to have.

Most stores retain the registry for a year or longer to allow added listings for holidays and the first anniversary.

Submitting Newspaper Announcements

Check with your local newspaper or newspapers to see what their policy is on printing announcements. Some print engagement and wedding announcements, some print only wedding announcements, and others do not print either.

To submit an announcement, refer to the specific form and information used in previous issues. Neatly type an announcement using the same form. At the top, type "CONTACT:" with your name, address, and telephone number following. Skip a few spaces and type "FOR IMMEDI-

ATE RELEASE" or "FOR RELEASE AFTER (date)." Then begin the notice. Mail the notice and a black and white photo, if they use them, to the paper or hand deliver them if you feel personal contact might help ensure placement.

CHAPTER THREE
Trousseau Treasures

In years past, young ladies kept hope chests in which they assembled a trousseau, including clothing and linens, in preparation for their future marriage. The hope chest and trousseau are both lovely traditions that some people still follow today.

Even without a hope chest, however, most brides receive some trousseau items from friends and relatives at showers or as special gifts. The bride and her mother will often add to the trousseau, which will include all of the new household and personal items the bride will take with her when she begins married life.

Trousseau objects are often of a romantic nature, adorned with ruffles, ribbons, lace, and flowers. They're also great items for featuring special needlework or other sewing and crafting skills that the bride will treasure for years to come.

Making Something Special

Whether you make a project yourself or simply embellish something that's already constructed, the effort you put into the item can elevate it from plain to very special.

Easy appliqué

This is one of the speediest decorative options, especially when you use paper-backed fusible web:

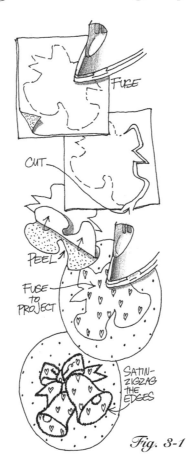

Fig. 3-1

1. Trace or draw the appliqué design on the paper side of the web. (If the image is directional, such as the letter "C," be sure to reverse it so that it will be positioned correctly when applied to the fabric.)

2. Fuse the web to the wrong side of the appliqué fabric, following the manufacturer's instructions, and let it cool. (Fig. 3-1)

3. Cut out the appliqué following the traced outline.

4. Peel the paper backing off the appliqué, position the design on the project, and fuse it in place.

5. Using a satin-length zigzag, sew over the raw edges of the

appliqué, permanently stitching it to the fabric underneath.

Machine embroidery and monogramming

When you decorate linens or household items for the trousseau, you have an excellent opportunity to get the most out of your sewing machine. Most of today's computerized models have lettering capabilities. If you have one that does, program it to sew a monogram or name and personalize your project. Many machines have other decorative options as well. Even the simplest decorative stitch can add interest and make an item unique.

If you have a sewing machine without programming capabilities, you can still embroider using free-machine embroidery with the presser foot removed and the feed dogs lowered or covered. If you haven't tried it, this technique takes a little practice, but you may enjoy it so much that you'll become an enthusiast.

Whether you're embroidering with programmed machine stitches or using the free-machine method, it helps to stabilize the fabric in an embroidery hoop designed specifically for machine embroidery. (Fig. 3-2)

Follow these general tips for successful machine embroidery:

🍃 Before you begin working on a project, always test first using the same design and thread on scraps of the project fabric.

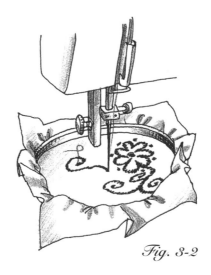

Fig. 3-2

🍃 An open-toed embroidery foot gives better visibility for machine embroidery, but a regular embroidery foot will hold the fabric more securely. The foot should have a scoop on the underside to allow it to climb easily over the buildup of thread.

🍃 Use the smallest size of machine needle that won't cause skipped stitches and that works with the thickness of the thread. Always begin with a sharp new needle.

🍃 Stitch slowly to reduce puckering and skipped stitches.

🍃 Stabilize the underside of the fabric if you are having problems with tunneling and puckering. Use interfacing, tear-away stabilizer, or paper.

🍃 Loosen the machine's upper and lower tensions as necessary to perfect the stitch.

Other embellishment options

If you have special sewing or crafting skills, show them off in the trousseau. Hand embroidery,

machine embroidery, needlepoint, cross stitch, knitting, crocheting, quilting, and decorative painting or stenciling are only a few examples of what you may choose to do. See page 126 for tips on making rosettes and page 129 for adding other finishing touches.

> **"***Make milliner's roses out of sheer tricot or satin ribbon to trim lingerie or other trousseau items:*
>
> *1. Cut a strip on the crossgrain 3" to 4" wide and about 15" long. Fold the strip in half lengthwise, wrong sides together, and trim the strip so it looks like a triangle.*
>
> *2. Run a gathering thread along the cut edges.*
>
> *3. Gather and roll the small end to make the center; tack securely.*
>
> *4. Repeat until most of the strip is gathered, rolled, and tacked. Fold the raw end down to the gathered line and tack. You can also cover the raw edges with a small piece of fabric and add leaves.*
>
> *"Use faille or satin strips 8" to 9" wide and 45" to 54" long to make larger roses for shower decorations or to trim the back of wedding gowns.***"**
>
> *Claire Shaeffer*
> Claire Shaeffer's Fabric
> Sewing Guide

Use some of the following ideas to make trousseau treasures that are uniquely your own:

Throw pillows—Monogram or embroider a square of batiste or broadcloth. Top-stitch flat lace or trim to the cut edges, mitering the corners. Fuse or hand-sew the decorated square to the center of a pillow or pillow sham. (Or hand-sew a Battenberg or crocheted lace doily to the center.) Add matching lace to sham edges, if desired. (Fig. 3-3)

Fig. 3-3

Bed linens—Add machine embroidery, decorative machine stitching, or a satin-length zigzag over the hemline top-stitching on plain sheets and pillowcases. Or top-stitch crocheted lace or embroidered trim onto them.

Towels—Decorate plain towels and face cloths by top-stitching ribbon and lace to them. (First make narrow hems to finish any

raw edges on the trim.) Add machine embroidery, appliqués, or ribbon roses as decorative accents. (Fig. 3-4)

Fig. 3-4

Table linens—Make napkins and placemats, finishing the edges with decorative binding or serging. Add machine embroidery or cutwork. Embellish the edges and corners of purchased napkins and a tablecloth with matching lace or crocheted trim. A card-table cloth can be as simple as fringing or hemming the edges of a 45" fabric square.

Lingerie—Sew delicate items such as a camisole, slip, or nightgown that call for a less exacting fit. Embroider or appliqué them to add romantic touches and help the bride feel extra special.

Other personal items—Use patterns, kits, or your own designs to make special items that the new couple will enjoy taking into married life. The projects in the remainder of this chapter should give you some inspiration.

"*Friendship quilts are a wonderful tradition and a way to remember the names and faces of those people who made your wedding memorable. In today's busy world, people are often too busy to make a block for a quilt top, and differing sewing skills can give a hodge-podge look to a collective quilt.*

"*A friend of mine solved this problem by having the guests at her daughter's wedding sign the quilt backing before the quilt was assembled. She stretched it out on a table at the wedding reception and asked a quilting friend to help answer questions and monitor the table. The backing was clamped to the table with binder clamps to hold it securely and make writing easier. The table was stocked with an assortment of permanent markers, including* fabric crayons. All of the guests, including children, were encouraged to sign the backing. Then it was used to finish the beautiful quilt my friend had made.

"It is the best of all possible solutions. On the bed, the quilt is a beautifully made, color-coordinated design. Its timeless design and colors will make it a treasure for generations. At the same time, the back displays hundreds of names and well wishes from family and friends and serves as an irreplaceable keepsake of a special day and special people."

Debra Wagner
Teach Yourself Machine Piecing and Quilting

Terrific Taffeta Pillows

Quickly make a pile of pillows to complement the couple's new living room or bedroom decor. (Fig. 3-5)

Fig. 3-5

MATERIALS NEEDED FOR EACH PILLOW

One pillow form (or purchased pillow)

One piece of taffeta twice the size of the pillow

A contrasting color of taffeta (or taffeta ribbon) for a bow

CUTTING DIRECTIONS

Make a pattern by measuring the pillow form and adding ¼" to all edges for seam allowances.

Cut two pieces of taffeta the size of the pattern.

HOW-TOS

Sew or serge all seams using ¼" allowances.

1. Place the taffeta pieces right sides together and seam the edges, leaving a large opening on one side for inserting the pillow.

2. Turn the fabric right side out and put in the pillow. Hand-sew the opening closed.

3. Make a tie from the contrasting fabric by serge-finishing with narrow rolled edges or sewing narrow double hems. (Fig. 3-6) You'll need a strip long enough to tie completely around the pillow plus another yard or so for the bow. Piece the strip if necessary.

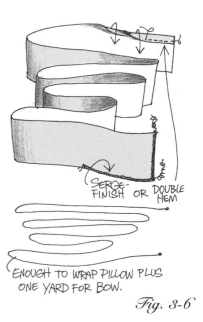

SERGE-FINISH OR DOUBLE HEM

ENOUGH TO WRAP PILLOW PLUS ONE YARD FOR BOW.

Fig. 3-6

4. Tie the ribbon around the pillow, forming a large bow in the center.

Elegant Embroidered Shams

Machine or hand embroidery on top of quilted satin makes these tie-on shams real attention-getters. (Fig. 3-7)

Fig. 3-7

MATERIALS NEEDED FOR EACH SHAM

One piece of quilted, double-faced satin twice the size of the pillow

Two yards of ⅜"-wide satin ribbon

A quilting stencil for the design

CUTTING DIRECTIONS

Make a pattern by measuring the pillow and adding 2" on one short end (includes a 1" hem) and 1" on the other three sides.

Using the pattern, cut two pieces of quilted satin.

HOW-TOS

Sew or serge all seams using ¼" allowances.

1. Embroider a stencilled design on the right side of one sham piece, centering it after temporarily folding back the 1" hem allowance.

2. With right sides together, seam both long edges and the one short end that will not be hemmed.

3. At the open end, turn ½" to the wrong side, then turn ½" again and top-stitch to form a hem.

4. Cut the ribbon into four equal lengths.

5. Position the ribbons right sides together with the sham with the ribbon edges near the outer hem edge. Sew across them on the hem top-stitching line. (Fig. 3-8)

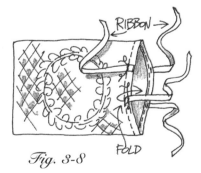

Fig. 3-8

6. Fold the ribbons at the stitching and top-stitch again close to the hem edge. Cut the loose ends on an angle to prevent fraying.

7. Insert the pillow and tie the sham closed with the ribbons.

Captivating Chiffon Kimono

Any bride will look alluring in this pretty wrap kimono with draped-front chiffon detailing. (Fig. 3-9)

Fig. 3-9

MATERIALS NEEDED

1⅞ yards of 45"-wide lace yardage, textured satin, or any lightweight drapable fabric

1⅛ yards of chiffon

CUTTING DIRECTIONS

Cut out the kimono, following the measurements in Figure 3-10.

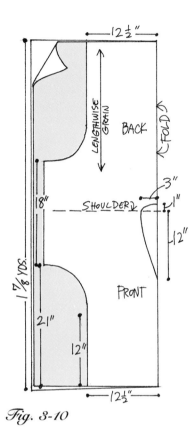

Fig. 3-10

Note: The kimono fits a medium size (36" to 38" hips). Alter the pattern by adding or subtracting ¾" to the side seams per size. Make any length adjustments at the lower edge.

Trim out the neckline opening and cut open the remainder of the center front along the fold-line.

Cut two chiffon rectangles for the draped front 16" wide by the length of the fabric.

HOW-TOS

Sew or serge all seams using ¼" allowances. When sewing, also clean-finish the hem and seam-allowance edges using a narrow zigzag or another finishing stitch.

1. Finish the sleeve hem edges using a serged rolled edge or a clean-finishing stitch.

2. Refold the kimono with right sides together, matching the side and sleeve underarm seams. Sew both sides and underarms.

3. Clean-finish or serge-finish the lower edge to match the sleeves.

4. Place the two chiffon rectangles right sides together and seam one short end to form one long strip.

5. With the chiffon seam at center back, measure to the lower edge on both sides and trim the chiffon to that measurement.

6. Fold both lower short ends of the chiffon strip in half, right sides together, and seam using a ½" allowance. If you're sewing instead of serging, trim the allowance to ¼" and clean-finish the edges.

7. Turn the chiffon right side out and pin it right sides together to the front and neckline edge, matching the raw edges and positioning the chiffon seam at the center back. (The chiffon will be ½" shorter than the kimono at the lower center-front edges.)

8. Fold the lower center-front edges over the chiffon to the right side. (Fig. 3-11) Seam the front and neckline edges. If you're sewing instead of serging, clean-finish the seam allowances together.

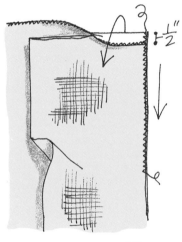

Fig. 3-11

9. Fold the lower and sleeve hems ½" to the wrong side and top-stitch them in place.

Handy Hideaway Hanger

Adorn lovely padded hangers to go along with the bride's new wardrobe. If sewing isn't your forté or you're in a hurry, simply purchase plain satin-covered hangers and add ribbon roses, bows, ribbons, and lace to make them prettier. (Fig. 3-12)

Fig. 3-12

MATERIALS NEEDED FOR EACH HANGER

⅓ yard of satin

⅓ yard of matching lining fabric

⅓ yard of fusible fleece

⅝ yard of paper-backed fusible web

2 yards of 2"-wide gathered lace

⅔ yard of ⅝"-wide satin ribbon

One matching 22" zipper

One large ribbon rose

Eight small ribbon roses

One matching plastic hanger

CUTTING DIRECTIONS

Make a cover pattern by tracing around the hanger. Add ½" around the top and sides and extend the bottom for a total height of 9". Curve out an opening at the center top. (Fig. 3-13)

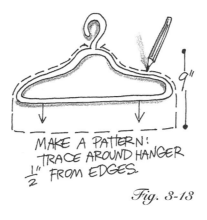

MAKE A PATTERN: TRACE AROUND HANGER ½" FROM EDGES.

Fig. 3-13

Cut one 45" by 12" rectangle each from the satin, fleece, and lining.

HOW-TOS

Sew or serge all seams using ¼" allowances.

1. Fuse the fleece to the wrong side of the satin rectangle.

2. Fuse paper-backed web to the wrong side of the lining fabric. Remove the paper and fuse the lining to the fleece rectangle.

3. Using the pattern you made, cut two cover pieces from the fused fabric. Finish the opening edges by turning ¼" to the wrong side and top-stitching (or serge-finishing with a narrow balanced stitch).

4. Press ½" to the wrong side at the lower edge of both cover pieces.

5. Lap and top-stitch one pressed edge close to the zipper teeth on the right side of the zipper. Sew the other cover piece opposite, aligning it with the first piece. (Fig. 3-14)

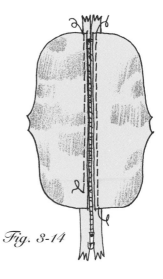

Fig. 3-14

6. Top-stitch the lace onto the right side of the fabric ⅜" from the zipper teeth, with the finished lace edge extending over the zipper and both ends extending ½" past the fabric. (Fig. 3-15) Repeat for the other side of the zipper.

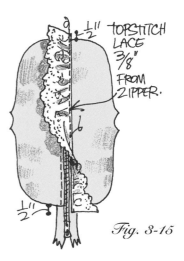

TOPSTITCH LACE ⅜" FROM ZIPPER.

Fig. 3-15

7. Unzip the zipper halfway. With the right sides together, fold the lace extensions back and seam the outer edges of the cover, being careful not to catch the lace in the stitching.

8. Turn the cover right side out. Fold the ½" lace extensions under and hand-sew the edges together.

9. Tie the satin ribbon into a bow and hand-sew it to the top of the cover at the center edge of the opening.

10. Tightly gather the straight edge of the remaining lace to form a rosette. Attach the larger ribbon rose to the center of the rosette and hand-tack it over the bow.

11. Hand-sew the smaller ribbon roses at random on both sides and place the cover on the hanger.

Dainty Doily Sachet

It's amazing that something so pretty can be this simple to make. Whip up several to keep the bride's dresser drawers freshly scented. (Fig. 3-16)

Fig. 3-16

MATERIALS NEEDED

One 7" white or off-white crocheted doily with scalloped edges (handmade or purchased)

One 6" circle of white tulle or netting

1½ yards of ⅛"-wide ribbon in a wedding color or a pretty pastel

Potpourri—colored to match or coordinate with the ribbon

One ribbon rose

A tapestry needle

How-Tos

1. Fold the netting circle in half and seam the cut edges using a ⅛" seam allowance and leaving an opening for filling.

2. Fill the netting firmly with potpourri and hand-sew the opening closed.

3. Fold the doily over the filled netting, stretching it, if necessary, to completely cover the netting edge. Align the scallops on the two doily layers. Thread the tapestry needle with the ribbon. Leaving 2" of ribbon extending, take one stitch into the doily to secure the end. (Fig. 3-17)

Fig. 3-17

4. Thread the ribbon through the openings in the doily, being careful not to twist it. Secure the opposite end by taking one stitch through the doily. Cut the ribbon, leaving 2" extending.

5. Knot both ribbon ends.

6. Tie the remaining ribbon into a bow and hand-sew it to the sachet. Hand-sew the ribbon rose over the bow center.

Pretty Potpourri Pillow

Add a touch of Victorian charm to the trousseau with a small pillow to hang in the boudoir. The dried-flower filling will softly scent the room. (Fig. 3-18)

Fig. 3-18

MATERIALS NEEDED

One 8" circle of satin

One 8" circle of organza

⅔ yard of 2½"-wide ruffled lace

One 4" lace doily

¾ yard ⅜"-wide satin ribbon

Dried flowers

HOW-TOS

Sew or serge all seams using 1/4" allowances.

1. Center the doily on the organza circle and machine or hand-sew them together.

2. Fold one end of the lace ½" to the wrong side. With right sides together, sew the lace to the edge of the organza circle. At the other end, fold the lace ½" to the right side and overlap the ends ½" to finish. (Fig. 3-19)

Fig. 3-19

3. Place the circles right sides together and seam the edges, leaving an opening for turning and stuffing. Be careful not to catch the loose lace in the stitching.

4. Turn the pillow right side out and fill it with dried flowers. Hand-sew the opening closed.

5. Cut the ribbon into two equal pieces. Tie one into a bow and hand-sew it at the upper edge of the doily.

6. Form a loop with the remaining ribbon, place it behind the lace at the upper edge, and machine stitch it in place.

Super-Simple Shoe Bag

Send the bride off on her honeymoon with a supply of pretty shoe bags. They'll also be wonderful when she organizes her new closets. (Fig. 3-20)

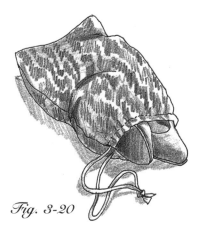

Fig. 3-20

MATERIALS NEEDED FOR EACH BAG

One 15½" by 18½" rectangle of quilted satin, moiré, or chintz

¾ yard of ⅛" satin cording

HOW-TOS

Sew or serge all seams using ¼" allowances.

1. Finish one long edge with serging or clean-finish it by turning ¼" to the wrong side and top-stitching.

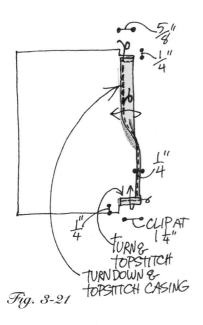

Fig. 3-21

2. Make a ¼" clip 1¼" from the finished edge on both short sides. (Fig. 3-21)

3. Turn the edges above the clips ¼" to the wrong side and top-stitch them in place.

4. To complete the casing, turn the long finished edge ⅝" to the wrong side and top-stitch along it.

5. Fold the rectangle in half crosswise, right sides together, and seam the side and bottom. If you're sewing instead of serging, finish the seam allowances together. Secure the ends well and turn the bag right side out.

6. Thread the satin cording through the casing and knot the ends together.

Scented Shoe Stuffer

The bride's shoes will stay fresh and sweet-smelling with these small potpourri sachets. (Fig. 3-22)

Fig. 3-22

MATERIALS NEEDED FOR TWO STUFFERS

¼ yard of moiré or plain taffeta

¾ yard of ¾"-wide ruffled lace

½ yard of ¼"-wide satin ribbon

Potpourri

CUTTING DIRECTIONS

Cut four 4" by 7" rectangles from the taffeta.

Round both corners on one short end of each rectangle.

HOW-TOS

Sew or serge all seams using ¼" allowances.

1. Finish the unrounded short edges with a serged rolled edge or turn ⅛" twice to the wrong side and top-stitch a hem.

2. Cut the lace into two equal lengths. Place each lace section right sides together with the cut edge of one rectangle, centering it at the rounded end. Baste, tapering the ends off the fabric 2½" from the unrounded corners. (Fig. 3-23)

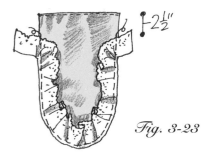

Fig. 3-23

3. Place the remaining rectangles right sides together over the stitched ones. Seam, following the basting stitches as a guide and being careful not to catch any of the loose lace in the stitching. Turn the fabric right side out.

4. Cut the ribbon into two equal lengths. Fold the sections in half and center one on the side of each stuffer, 1½" from the upper edge. Machine-sew the ribbons in place.

5. Firmly fill both bags with potpourri. Wrap the ribbon tightly around the stuffers, tying the ends in a bow. Hand-sew the bows in place, then hand-sew a ribbon rose at the center of both.

Lacy Lingerie Tote

Delicate lace detailing accents this pretty organizer. It's handy for lingerie, hosiery, and other small accessory items. (Fig. 3-24)

Fig. 3-24

MATERIALS NEEDED

⅔ yard of moiré or plain taffeta

⅓ yard of lightweight polyester fleece

⅔ yard of 1½"- to 2"-wide ruffled lace

2" of satin cording

One pearl ball button

CUTTING DIRECTIONS

Cut two 12" by 24" rectangles from the taffeta.

Cut one 12" by 24" rectangle from the fleece.

Using a plate as a guide, round the corners on one short end of each rectangle.

HOW-TOS

Sew or serge all seams using ¼" allowances.

1. On one taffeta rectangle, fold 9" of the unrounded short end to the right side. Mark the fold with a pin at both corners.

2. Unfold the rectangle and, beginning at one marking, baste the lace, right sides together, to the rounded end. Ease the lace to the fabric at both ends and finish at the opposite pin-marking. (Fig. 3-25)

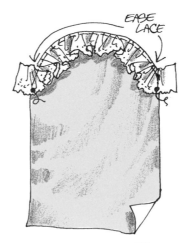

Fig. 3-25

3. Fold the satin cording into a loop and, with cut edges matching, baste the loop onto the center of the rounded edge over the lace. (Fig. 3-26)

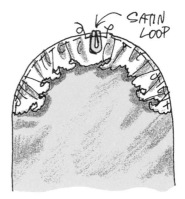

Fig. 3-26

4. With the taffeta right sides together and the fleece underneath, seam, leaving an opening in the short unfinished edge for turning. Be careful not to catch the loose lace in the stitching.

5. Turn the tote right side out. Edge-stitch the fabric along both short ends.

6. Fold up 9" of the plain end to form a pocket. Edge-stitch along both sides through all layers, securing the pocket sides.

7. Hand-sew the button in place.

For additional trousseau ideas and how-to instructions, see *Sew Sensational Gifts* and *Distinctive Serger Gifts & Crafts*.

CHAPTER FOUR

Parties, Parties, Parties

In the months before the wedding, you'll most likely be doing a balancing act. All of the planning and organization will vie for your time with the many prenuptial events that help to make the entire celebration so special and memorable.

Friends and families may want to honor the happy couple at a dinner or party. This is especially nice when one of the two is unknown to many of them.

Future in-laws are often eager to become better acquainted. And out-of-town guests will appreciate being entertained.

In the center of this social whirl, there's likely to be one or more showers, a rehearsal dinner, and other typical events such as an engagement party, bridesmaids' luncheon, and a bachelor party. This chapter presents some creative ideas to get through them in style.

Sanity Saver

Often close friends and relatives will have ideas about your wedding festivities that may differ from yours. Try to use sensitivity and tact to prevent any misunderstandings and make this a happy time for everyone.

The Big Announcement

The bride and groom have the option of announcing their engagement formally at a party or other special occasion or by simply telling close friends and family individually. If you do plan an engagement party, there are several options:

🕯 A cocktail party

🕯 An intimate dinner with close family and friends

🕯 Another gathering of many of those close to the couple. (Just be sure that if the event is honoring someone else, they are in on the announcement in advance and approve of it. You don't want to steal someone else's chance to shine.)

Traditionally, the future bride does not wear her engagement

ring until the engagement party. Any engagement announcements in local newspapers should appear after (or simultaneously with) the engagement party. The announcement at the event is often made in the form of a toast by the bride's father or another close friend or relative. The event is often hosted by the bride's parents, but other relatives, friends,

or the couple themselves may do so also.

An engagement party is one of the few wedding events that will work well as a surprise. Guests can be invited on the pretext of a normal dinner or party, then the announcement can be made at a strategic time.

Budget Helper

One couple we know took the event even one step further. As a second-time marriage for both, a weekend at the coast for those close to them became both an engagement party and a surprise wedding! It was a no-hassle, no-gift, no-worry, inexpensive, and truly memorable occasion.

Showers to Remember

The showers preceding a wedding can be lots of fun and also very helpful for the bride. They are typically a chance for the "girls" to get together and talk about the future while showering the bride with either personal or household items that will be helpful as she begins married life. Keep these general guidelines in mind:

🐦 A shower is usually a small, lighthearted, informal party that can be scheduled for any time of day or any day of the week. Showers are best given one to two months prior to the wedding, after the bride has registered and before she gets too busy with the last-minute rush.

🐦 Traditionally, friends or friends of the family (not relatives) host showers. If relatives wish to entertain, it is usually done at a coffee, tea, or luncheon where gifts are not expected.

🐦 If anyone is invited to more than one shower (attendants, relatives, close friends), the bride should tell them personally not to feel obligated to attend every event (but that they are very welcome to) and also that she does not expect them to give any more than one gift.

🐦 The bride should give each shower hostess an accurate list of the guests' names and addresses well in advance. She should later give her a small gift and send a sincere thank-you note. If the hostess gift will be a flower arrangement for the shower, the hostess needs to be told in advance.

🐦 A surprise shower is usually too difficult to plan, because the bride will probably need to help with the guest list, being sure no one is left out unintentionally. It is also customary that anyone invited to a shower also will receive a wedding invitation.

🐦 One entertaining modern trend is a shower to which the groom, male friends, and spouses are also invited. To make it more interesting for the men, the event could be a cocktail party, barbecue, or any other activity of mutual interest.

🐦 Invitations should be sent two to three weeks prior to the shower, announcing the shower theme if there is one. A note as to where the bride is registered may be included or the hostess may simply tell those who inquire.

🐦 The bride and the gifts given to her should be the focus of the event. The group may even choose to give one large gift, asking each guest to contribute.

🐦 Shower games are popular only in some areas and social circles and are avoided in others. A shower shouldn't last too long,

Budget Helper

Add another fun element to any shower with a kit and caboodle centerpiece. Let each guest know on the invitation to bring an anonymous additional gift of great use but little value, even including words of advice. Everything will be presented together (in a pretty basket, hung from a miniature tree, or as part of a creative arrangement). This can be truly amusing for a very small expense. (Fig. 4-1)

Fig. 4-1

leaving the bride time to get back to all of her pressing tasks.

🐦 In the past, showers were not given for second marriages, but they're much more acceptable today and sometimes very much needed. A combined gift of a more costly item, gift certificates, items of special interest to the couple, and even lingerie are all appropriate.

Selecting a shower theme

A popular custom today is to choose a theme for the shower to focus the type of gifts given. If you confer with the bride before choosing a theme, she won't be deluged with the same type of gifts at several different showers. Consider these theme options or use your creativity for one that will be most helpful for the couple:

Room shower—Each invited guest brings a gift for a specific room in the house. Assign the rooms when sending the invitations.

Entertainment shower—Give a VCR, videotapes, CDs, tickets to a special event, or other related items. This theme is especially good for a couple who already has lots of household items.

Travel shower—Gifts can include luggage, a weekend getaway, lingerie bags, garment bags, and cosmetic bags.

Service shower—Each guest will present the bride with a "labor of love," giving a promise of their own time, talents, and energy instead of gifts. The future "gift certificates" could be for such things as a catered dinner party or luncheon, yard work, housecleaning, or sewing.

Covered dish shower—Ask the guests to bring covered dishes for a potluck. Afterward, the dishes are washed and given to the bride.

Quilting shower—Have each guest bring a decorated square with a motif relating to the cou-

ple. For continuity, send each invitee a fabric square along with the invitation. At the shower, the guests can assemble the quilt.

Kitchen shower—This type of shower is especially helpful for a bride who is on her own for the first time. Consider including specific information with each invitation, such as where the bride is registered, her color choices, any brand preferences, and the types of food the couple prefers.

Linen shower—Similar to the kitchen shower, this theme works well for a young bride. Although it is best to check her registry for what she needs, it is a perfect opportunity for guests to show off their needlework and sewing skills.

Lingerie or personal shower—Enclose the bride's sizes in the invitation, and mention her favorite colors and styles if you wish. Appropriate gifts could be teddies, half-slips, and nightgowns, as well as closet or drawer organizers.

Alphabet shower—Assign each guest a different letter of the alphabet when the invitations are sent (or letters from the bride's

and groom's names). Each gift should begin with the assigned letter.

Around-the-clock shower—Send out invitations asking each guest to bring a gift that would be used at a specific time of day. For example, a gift for 9:00 AM could have something to do with breakfast. A gift for midnight could be lingerie. Ask each guest to enclose a note or poem explaining why they chose the gift.

Paper shower—Each guest is asked to give a gift made of paper, such as stationery, prints for framing, photograph albums, books, or magazine subscriptions.

Special meal shower—This theme is an excellent one for both men and women. Choose a barbecue, pasta feast, gourmet dinner, or another meal the couple will appreciate. Guests come for the meal and bring gifts related to cooking it.

Special interest shower—If the bride has a special interest such as gardening or crafting, it can be selected as a shower theme. (Fig. 4-2) This is another good idea for older or second-

Fig. 4-2

time brides who already have most necessities.

Holiday shower—When you choose this theme, the bride receives a number of items she'll greatly appreciate and probably wouldn't buy for herself. Assign different holidays to each guest—Christmas, Easter, Fourth of July, Halloween, and Thanksgiving, for example. This theme works especially well for a group of skilled crafters or sewing enthusiasts.

Recipe and grocery shower—A young bride starting married life on a limited income will really appreciate this theme. Not only do guests bring one of their favorite recipes, they also help stock her cupboards for the months ahead.

Decorations

Shower decorations are an excellent way of adding to the festivity of the occasion. They're often designed to follow the chosen theme, so you can become as creative as your skill and imagination permit. All-purpose decorations that lend themselves to many themes are also popular.

The following fast and simple tie-on rosettes, bows, and skirts can enhance your other theme-oriented decorations.

"A covered wooden rolling pin is the perfect bridal shower decoration. A cover of satins, laces, and ribbons—all matching the bridal dress and the wedding colors—is added for decoration. The cover can be quilted and beaded or even embellished with three-dimensional lace or fabric flowers. It should be a wonderful excess of frills and ribbons, made in a tube that closely fits the body of the rolling pin. Use ribbon drawstrings to tie the ends.

"During the shower, remove the cover and have the guests sign the rolling pin with a permanent marker. Then seal it with a coat of polyurethane and give it to the bride after the wedding as a keepsake.

"My mother and a number of my aunts still own their rolling pins from their own showers during the 1940s. (Then they were sealed with varnish!) As an adult, it is wonderful for me to look on a signed rolling pin and see the names of my great aunts and long-lost relatives. When guest books have been long ago packed away and forgotten, the rolling pin is still kept in the kitchen drawer where it is seen, used (if only occasionally), and cherished"

Debra Wagner
Teach Yourself Machine Piecing and Quilting

Tie-on Lace Rosettes

Quickly make these showy rosettes to embellish glass stems, a cake knife, and flower arrangements. (Fig. 4-3)

Fig. 4-3

MATERIALS NEEDED FOR TWO ROSETTES

2 to 3 yards of 2½"- to 3"-wide flat lace with one scalloped edge

Four yards of ⅛"-wide matching or contrasting satin ribbon

Two yards of ¼"-wide satin ribbon to match the ⅛"-wide ribbon (the length depends on what the rosette will be tied to)

⅔ yard of pearl beading

Two large ribbon roses

A glue gun or quick-drying craft glue

CUTTING DIRECTIONS

Cut the lace, ribbon, and pearls into two equal lengths each.

HOW-TOS FOR EACH ROSETTE

1. Using a sewing machine, serger, or long running hand-stitch, gather the straight edge of one piece of the lace. Pull the threads to gather the lace tightly, then knot securely. Distribute the gathers evenly.

2. Tie one piece of the ⅛"-wide ribbon into a multiple bow and glue it to the center of the rosette. (Fig. 4-4)

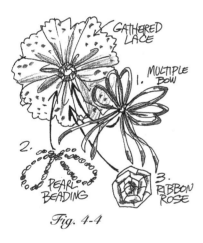

Fig. 4-4

3. Arrange one strand of pearls into two loops and glue it over the bow. Then glue a ribbon rose on top.

4. Glue the center of a ¼"-wide ribbon section to the center back of the rosette for the ties.

Tie-on Lace Bows

Use these simple no-sew decorations anywhere you would the lace rosettes, including tablecloth corners, napkins, and serving dishes. (Fig. 4-5)

Fig. 4-5

MATERIALS NEEDED FOR TWO BOWS

1 yard of 2½"-wide flat lace scalloped on both sides
⅔ yard of pearl beading
1⅓ yard of ¼"-wide satin ribbon
A glue gun or quick-drying craft glue

CUTTING DIRECTIONS

Cut both the lace and pearls into two equal lengths.

Cut the ribbon into two 18" lengths and two 6" lengths.

HOW-TOS FOR EACH BOW

1. Fold one lace piece into thirds. (Fig. 4-6)

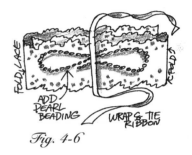

Fig. 4-6

2. Arrange one pearl strand into two loops and glue it to the center front of the lace.

3. Center and tie one 18" length of ribbon securely over the lace, catching the ends of the pearls. Knot the ribbon securely at the back of the bow.

4. Tie a 6" length of ribbon into a bow and glue it over the pearl ends on the front of the bow.

Tie-on Lace Skirts

Embellish the base of candlesticks or vases with dainty wrap and tie skirts. Just make a few quick stitches and they're done! (Fig. 4-7)

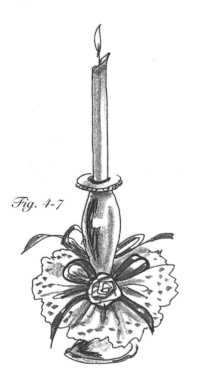

Fig. 4-7

MATERIALS NEEDED FOR TWO SKIRTS

⅞ yard of flat lace 2" to 4" wide with one straight edge and a design open enough so that ⅛"-wide ribbon can be threaded through it near the straight edge (if the object you'll be tying the skirt around has a circumference of more than 6", purchase enough lace to equal about 3 times the circumference)

2¼ yards of ⅛"-wide matching or contrasting satin ribbon

One large matching or contrasting ribbon rose

A tapestry needle

A glue gun or quick-drying craft glue

CUTTING DIRECTIONS

Cut the lace into two equal lengths.

Cut two 12" lengths of ribbon, then cut the remaining ribbon into two equal lengths.

HOW-TOS FOR EACH SKIRT

1. Thread the tapestry needle with one longer piece of ribbon and weave it through holes in the lace, close to the straight edge. (Fig. 4-8) Pull up the ends to gather the skirt.

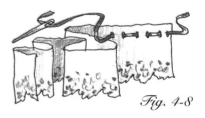

Fig. 4-8

2. Tie a 12" length of ribbon into a bow and glue it at the top of the skirt, opposite the cut edges.

3. Glue a ribbon rose over the bow.

4. Tie on the skirt, forming a bow with the ribbon ends.

Refreshments

The food served at a shower can vary widely, depending upon the type of shower you're giving, the time of day, and personal preferences. Try to serve food that is light and easy to eat, especially if the guests won't be seated at a table. Also consider coordinating the food with the shower theme.

Punch is served at many showers as a refreshing accompaniment to the food. With a little planning, you may even want to use it to help carry out the wedding colors, if you're using them in your decorations.

When serving punch, keep in mind these ideas for making it more festive and tasty:

Make a decorative ice ring by placing fresh fruit in the bottom of a mold that is smaller than the punch bowl. (Also consider using mint leaves, herbs, or other colorful garnishes.) Add water to barely cover the fruit and freeze. Then add additional water and freeze again. Before placing the ring in the punch, allow it to stand for 10 or 15 minutes to thaw slightly so it can be removed from the mold easily.

Add ice cubes made of soda or ginger ale. Add a piece of fruit or a maraschino cherry to each cube for color.

For an added zing, substitute champagne or white wine for some of the other beverages in the punch.

Budget Helper

To extend the amount of punch if you are running low, add additional lemon-lime soda, ginger ale, or champagne.

Freeze ice blocks instead of cubes to keep the punch from becoming too diluted. Use half-gallon paper milk cartons and simply peel the carton away before serving each block.

To avoid diluting the punch, mix some of the recipe ahead of time and freeze it into cubes or a ring instead of making the ice from water.

Chill all punch ingredients before combining them. Add any carbonated beverages just before serving.

Try the following chilled punch recipes as a pleasing refreshment at any of the wedding events.

CRANBERRY PUNCH—

(Makes about thirty-six ½-cup servings)

1 quart cranberry juice

1 (46-ounce) can pineapple juice

1 (6-ounce) can frozen lemonade concentrate

¾ cup sugar

2 (28-ounce) bottles lemon-lime soda or ginger ale

Combine all ingredients except the soda or ginger ale in a punch bowl and chill. Just before serving, add the soda. Also add a garnish of lemon slices, a fruit ice ring, or scoops of lemon or pineapple sherbet, if desired.

SPARKLING PUNCH—

(Makes about fifty ½-cup servings)

4 (6-ounce) cans frozen lemonade concentrate

4 (9.6-ounce) cans frozen pineapple juice

1½ quarts cold water

2 quarts sparkling water

3 quarts ginger ale

Slices of fresh fruit

Combine the juices and water, then chill. Just before serving, add the ginger ale and sparkling water. For extra interest, add ice cubes made from fruit juice or ginger ale or put in scoops of lemon, orange, or lime sherbet. For a champagne punch, substitute champagne for the ginger ale and sparkling water.

QUICK PARTY PUNCH—

(Makes about thirty-six ½-cup servings)

Two quarts lime sherbet

3 (1-liter) bottles lemon-lime soda or ginger ale

Just before serving, scoop softened sherbet into the punch bowl. Slowly pour the soda or ginger ale over the sherbet. For extra color, add lemon-lime soda ice cubes with maraschino cherries in each or a fresh fruit ice ring, if desired.

Shower traditions

With the wide variety of clever showers being given today, very few "must do" traditions need to be observed. One tradition, however, is the opening of presents brought by the guests. To help this go smoothly, the bride should enlist the help of one of her attendants or a close friend to record each gift and who it is from. Someone else should be designated to take photos.

Another friend often helps the bride with the ribbons and wrapping paper. At many showers, the bows are gathered into a "bouquet" that can be used during the rehearsal. Cross-score the center of a paper plate and feed the ribbon tails through; or attach the bows to the plate with transparent tape. (Fig. 4-9)

Fig. 4-9

Another option for saving the ribbons and bows is to put them inside a see-through lace heart.

Heart-shaped Ribbon Saver

Fill this charming little bag with the ribbons and bows collected during the shower. Make the heart smaller or larger, if necessary, to accommodate the number of guests attending. (Fig. 4-10)

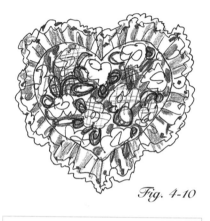

Fig. 4-10

MATERIALS NEEDED

½ yard of sheer lace

1½ yards of 2½"- to 3"-wide matching scalloped ruffled lace

1⅓ yards of ¼"-wide matching satin ribbon

CUTTING DIRECTIONS

Cut two hearts of sheer lace, following the pattern grid. (Fig. 4-11)

Cut the ribbon into six 8" lengths.

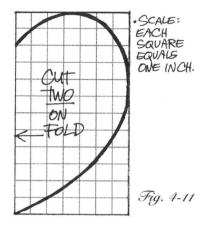

Fig. 4-11

HOW-TOS

Sew or serge all seams using ¼" allowances.

1. Fold one lace heart in half lengthwise and cut it into two equal pieces.

2. Top-stitch a narrow hem on the straight edges of both pieces.

3. On one half of the divided heart, position ribbon ties 2" from the top, directly in the center, and 2" from the bottom. (Fig. 4-12) Fold the ends ⅜" to the wrong side and place them against the right side of the hemmed edge with the ribbons extending toward the center. Top-stitch each one to the lace.

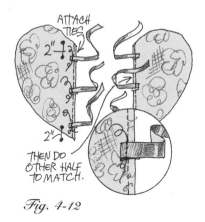

Fig. 4-12

4. Top-stitch the remaining ribbons to the other half of the heart, aligning them with the ribbons on the first piece.

5. On one end of the gathered lace, fold ½" to the wrong side and place it right sides together with the undivided heart, beginning at the point and matching the cut edges. Seam the lace to the heart, finishing by folding the opposite end ½" to the right side and overlapping the beginning end ¾", easing around the point and pulling the fold of the underlayer out of the way. (Fig. 4-13)

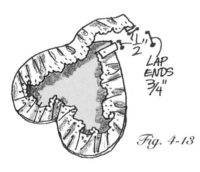

Fig. 4-13

6. Place the divided heart right sides together with the lace-trimmed heart, with the lace ruffle and ribbons between. Lap the upper and lower hemmed edges of the divided heart ¼". Seam the hearts together around the outer edges, being careful not to catch the loose ribbon ends in the stitching.

7. Turn the finished bag right side out. Tie the heart closed after the ribbons and bows are inserted.

Gifts and Packaging

It is often difficult to find the "perfect" shower gift. The thought and effort you put into the gift and its presentation will help make it more special. When considering your gift, take into account the couple's tastes, as well as the following:

🕭 What are their favorite colors?

🕭 Do they have a defined lifestyle—formal, sophisticated, outdoor, casual, western?

🕭 Does either the bride or groom like to cook? What type of foods are their favorites?

> **"** My husband and I assembled a fun gift for a friend's wedding by buying regional food specialties as we drove from Michigan to California and presented them all in a pretty box. This works very well for a blended family that already has household essentials. **"**
>
> *Marilyn Green*
> The Button Lover's Book

🕭 What special interests, hobbies, and sports do they enjoy?

🕭 What type of home will they live in—apartment, condo, house, military, city living, rural?

🕭 Do they enjoy interior decorating? What type of decor will they have in their home?

(If you wish, it may be helpful to include a summary of answers to the above list with the shower invitation.)

Budget Helper

To make a gift more memorable, construct it yourself or add your own personal touch to a purchased gift. Many times, in addition to being one-of-a-kind, this type of gift can save you money.

Keep in mind that not all home-created gifts will be appreciated by another person, so consider the recipient's tastes. Even if you don't display your creativity in making or embellishing the gift, put it to work in the wrapping or presentation.

A gift container can be your contribution to creativity without having to make the gift. The container itself will be part of the gift. Add decorative touches and lots of colorful tissue. Perhaps one of the following ideas will work for you:

🕭 Purchase plain gift bags available at craft stores and personalize them by painting designs or monograms or adding bows and flowers. (Fig. 4-14)

Fig. 4-14

🍃 Give an assorted garden gift in a terra-cotta pot or saucer. Include gloves, trowels, seeds, bulbs, potted plants, and/or a hat.

🍃 Collect an assortment of pasta paraphernalia and present it in a large colander lined with a checked luncheon cloth or towel. Various types of pasta, a garlic keeper and press, a pasta server, a cheese grater, a pasta recipe book, and jars of special sauces are all possible inclusions.

🍃 Wrap a collection of bath items in a large bath towel. Components could include additional towels, a matching shower curtain, bath oils and brushes, sponges, soaps, and accessory items such as a tissue holder or soap dish.

🍃 Cover a hat box and fill it with a unique dried arrangement or a handmade throw.

🍃 Use any type of basket, either plain or decorated, to present an assortment appropriate for the bride's or couple's tastes, interests, and needs. Possible groupings include kitchen utensils, spices, everyday kitchen linens, coffees and related items, gourmet cooking needs, and picnic items. (Fig. 4-15)

Fig. 4-15

DECORATE A BASKET—

Baskets are available in different shapes, sizes, and quality. Select a basket appropriate for the grouping of items you are giving. Keep in mind that a smaller basket completely filled is better than a larger basket that appears only half-full.

> ## Budget Helper
>
> *Recycle a basket, if you wish— a coat of spray paint is an easy coverup and can complement the colors you're using. After painting, you may also wish to add a personal touch by painting or decoupaging a design.*

A glue gun is an invaluable tool when decorating baskets. They are quite inexpensive and easy to use (follow the manufacturer's instructions), and the glue dries quickly. Use one to attach lightweight dried or silk flowers,

ribbons, bows, and other embellishments with minimum effort. (Heavier items should be tied or wired into place and then glued.) If any of the decorative items are meant to be taken off the basket and reused, attach them with wire or pins instead of glue. See page 130 for more glue gun tips.

Another creative way to decorate a basket is to cover the outside with fabric. Choose a fabric and color to coordinate with the gift assortment. Or you can quickly add a fabric skirt—a hemmed and gathered strip of fabric, glued to the basket rim. To make a fabric skirt:

1. Measure the circumference of the basket and determine the length of the skirt. Cut a rectangle of fabric twice the circumference by the skirt length plus 1". (Fig. 4-16) Piece the strip if necessary. *Optional:* Consider using wide gathered lace for the skirt, eliminating the hemming and gathering.

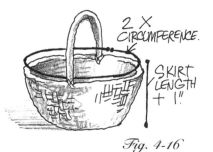
Fig. 4-16

2. Sew or serge the short ends of the rectangle together.

3. Hem the fabric circle by pressing ¼" to the wrong side twice on both long edges and then top-stitching. (Fig. 4-17)

Fig. 4-17

4. Using a sewing machine or serger, gather one long edge of the circle and glue it to the basket rim.

Embellish a basket handle simply by wrapping a ribbon around it, gluing in several places to keep it attached. You may choose to use several strands of different colors for added interest. Or wrap a long strip of tulle around the handle and tie the ends into bows at the sides (see Fig. 4-19). You can also wrap ribbon or garlands (with beads or shiny stars) over the tulle. Then glue on ribbon bows, flowers, or pearl beading for extra ornamentation.

WRAP A BASKET—

Use clear or colored cellophane to wrap the entire basket. Tie the edges together with a large bow. If you wish, wrap some of the gifts individually as well before putting them into the basket. (Fig. 4-18)

Fig. 4-18

LINE A BASKET—

The simplest basket lining is a napkin, luncheon cloth, or pinked fabric square. Other options include:

🍃 Metallic lamé fabric, simply serge-finished or narrow hemmed, to add elegance.

🍃 Colored cellophane, colored foil, or tissue paper to add color to the basket.

🍃 Paper confetti or shredded raffia, available at craft stores.

🍃 Spanish moss purchased inexpensively at craft or plant stores.

🍃 A hand towel or finger-towel (especially appropriate for a bathroom basket).

🍃 A custom fabric liner—see the following instructions.

Custom-lined Gift Basket

Add a simple liner to dress up any gift basket, using a fabric chosen to complement the gift. (Fig. 4-19)

Fig. 4-19

MATERIALS NEEDED

One basket

One fabric rectangle (for the liner), a little larger than the inside of the basket

One fabric rectangle (for the ruffle), cut to the measurements below

A glue gun

CUTTING DIRECTIONS

Place the fabric rectangle into the basket and arrange it to fit. Mark around the upper edge with chalk or an air-erasable marking pen. Remove the fabric, even up the markings, and cut, adding 1⅜" for an overhang and seam allowance. (Fig. 4-20)

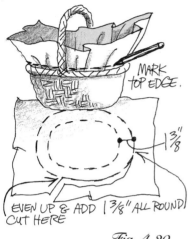

MARK TOP EDGE.

3/8"

(EVEN UP & ADD 1⅜" ALL ROUND)
CUT HERE

Fig. 4-20

Measure the upper edge of the liner and cut one strip of fabric twice this measurement by the desired ruffle width plus ⅝".

How-Tos

1. Using a sewing machine or serger, seam the ruffle strip into a circle, with the short ends right sides together.

2. Hem one long edge of the ruffle by pressing ¼" to the wrong side twice and top-stitching. (Or serge-finish using a rolled edge and trimming ¼".)

3. Gather the other edge of the ruffle (with the sewing machine or serger) to fit the upper edge of the liner piece.

4. Sew or serge the ruffle to the liner with right sides together and a ⅜" seam allowance.

5. Arrange the liner in the basket, right side up, allowing the edges to extend about 1" over the basket rim. Glue the liner in place.

6. Embellish the basket handle using some of the tips on page 129.

A Bridesmaids' Get-Together

Although a prewedding event for the bride and her attendants is not mandatory, it can be an excellent way for any of them who don't know each other to get acquainted. If you choose to have one, hold the get-together sometime during the last week before the wedding. Here are several options:

LUNCHEON—

Traditionally hosted by the bride or her mother to thank the attendants, a bridesmaids' luncheon can also be given by the groom's mother or another close relative or friend. Because of today's hectic pace, the luncheon is often held in a restaurant or other public place so that no one has to do much work. In addition to the attendants, both mothers should be invited. You may also invite the mothers of the flower girl and ring bearer, the flower girl herself if she's not too young, and any other close relatives and friends. The luncheon should be a very pleasant break from the flurry of activities during the wedding week. The bride may choose to give gifts to her attendants at this time, especially if it is a small, intimate party (she can also wait until the rehearsal dinner).

Budget Helper

If a morning event fits better into everyone's schedule, an informal breakfast or brunch can serve the same function as a bridesmaids' luncheon— often with less hassle and expense.

BEAUTY BASH—

The bride and her attendants may choose to get together at a local club, spa, or health resort for manicures, facials, or other beauty treatments before the wedding. The bride may host or the attendants may want to select and pay for their own specific choices. This can be a fun time-out and everyone will look great for the wedding.

*T*rousseau treasures, featured
in Chapter 3, help get the marriage off to an elegant start.
Sewn or crafted by relatives,
friends, or by the bride herself,
they can be romantic items or
for special household use.

*O*ne of the most appreciated shower gifts is an assortment of useful items that the bride or couple probably wouldn't already own. A decorated basket or bag makes a lovely gift container and is reusable, too. See Chapter 4 for more ideas.

A simple and inexpensive way to add a personal touch to the wedding is to make some or all of the accessories. Chapter 6 gives ideas for headpieces, veils, petticoats, and much more.

The bridal gown is usually a glamorous focal point for the wedding ceremony. Chapter 5 outlines how and where to find the right gown for every bride, whether it is purchased, made at home or by a dressmaker, borrowed, or rented.

*C*hapter 7 spells out how to coordinate all the members of the wedding party, including apparel and accessories, and who has responsibility for what. Step-by-step instructions for a flower girl's basket and ring bearer's pillow are also included.

Create the perfect wedding setting by following the tips in Chapter 8. Whether the event is held at home, in a church or other building, or out of doors, you can help set the mood with flowers, candles, and other romantic touches.

Celebrate the happy occasion at a reception to remember. Using the ideas in Chapter 8, you can easily put together a gala affair—from refreshments and decorations to the smallest incidentals.

When the festive events are over, hold onto the memories by making simple projects reminiscent of the wedding. Learn how to preserve the gown and flowers, plus get simple instructions for five delightful remembrances in Chapter 9.

GIRLS' NIGHT OUT—

If the guys will have a bachelor party, why can't the girls have their own? Using this logic, many brides now choose to have a "last night out on the town" as a single person with their closest friends. The event can be hosted by the maid of honor, but is often dutch treat. It's best held several days before the wedding so there's recovery time from any late-night partying, usually on the same night as the bachelor party.

The Boys' Night Out

A bachelor party is a last chance for the groom to party with his male friends as a single man. Although bachelor parties are often looked upon as wild affairs, today many grooms are opting for a quieter time. Attending a sporting event, a poker party at someone's home, or an evening of darts at the local pub can all be fun, depending on the groom's interests and personality.

The party can be hosted by the best man, another close relative or friend, or the groom himself. In the past, the bride was *never* to show up at the bachelor party. But today, some couples are combining it with a girls' night out or are meeting somewhere later in the evening. If lots of singles are involved, a combined party can give all of the participants a good opportunity to get better acquainted.

You're Almost There: The Rehearsal Dinner

This event is usually held the evening before the wedding, right after the rehearsal. Traditionally, it is a way for the groom's family to thank the bride's family for their generosity in putting on the wedding, but it can be hosted by anyone involved. It can be as formal or casual as you choose—anything from an elaborate dinner to an outdoor barbecue or pizza party.

Those invited in addition to the bride and groom may include their parents, each attendant with a spouse or friend, grandparents, the officiant, musicians, and any other relatives or friends who have traveled distances or are very close to the couple.

Planning the dinner

This event needs to be carefully planned and organized. The place must be chosen and reserved in advance and invitations should be sent out approximately three weeks ahead of time. If some of the guests haven't yet met, this is a good place to introduce them. For a more formal dinner, you'll also want to arrange the seating, so have place cards prepared and put out ahead of time.

You may choose a theme for this event, just as you would for the reception, but it's best to try not to outshine the events planned for the next day. Some find it entertaining to show photos, slides, or a video of the bride and groom in their younger days. And toasts are always in order, with either the host or best man beginning, followed by the groom, the bride, and any other friend or relative who wishes to participate.

Thanking those involved

The toasts are one way for the bride and groom to thank those people who are participating in their celebration and should be thought through in advance so that no one is omitted. If the couple has not already given gifts to their attendants, they can do so at the dinner—most often unobtrusively at their place settings.

The gifts are often personalized and should be something lasting, memorable, or sentimental to reflect the importance of the occasion. They can be wrapped using the wedding colors or, for the women, enclosed in boxes covered with fabric matching the wedding or bridesmaids' dresses.

Appropriate gifts for the bridesmaids include jewelry (perhaps in a jewelry box), a picture frame, dressing-table set, perfume atomizer, Victorian box, personalized stationery, or anything monogrammed.

> **"***Rescue the scraps of lace and fabrics left over from the wedding gown and dresses and use them to trim a sweatshirt. This could be a gift idea for bridal attendants, the bride, or family members. They'll enjoy wearing memories of the wedding on a casual, comfortable garment once the wedding is over.***"**
>
> *Mary Mulari*
> Sweatshirts with Style

Personalized Note Cards

Use your creativity to decorate a set of note cards for each bridesmaid, choosing colors, fabric, and trims to coordinate with the wedding. They'll be both an unusual remembrance and a useful gift. (Fig. 4-21)

Fig. 4-21

MATERIALS NEEDED

One set of plain note cards and envelopes, either single-layer or folded.

Scraps of fabric and trim from the wedding gown, bridesmaids' dresses, or decorations (because you'll be fusing, avoid open laces)

Paper-backed fusible transfer web

6" of 1/16"- or 1/8"-wide satin ribbon for each card

A glue gun or quick-drying craft glue

Optional: Dimensional fabric paint to match the card stock

CUTTING DIRECTIONS FOR EACH CARD

Fuse the web to the wrong side of the fabric and/or trim, using the method on page 31.

Draw three hearts on the paper backing, one of each size. Follow the pattern given (Fig. 4-22) or choose another shape. Use assorted fabrics for an interesting contrast.

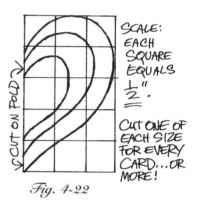

SCALE: EACH SQUARE EQUALS 1/2".

CUT ON FOLD

CUT ONE OF EACH SIZE FOR EVERY CARD...OR MORE!

Fig. 4-22

HOW-TOS

1. Fuse the hearts to the upper left corner of a single-layer note card or to the center front of a fold-over card.

2. *Optional:* Cover the edges of each heart with dimensional fabric paint. Be sure to follow the manufacturer's instructions and practice first.

3. Tie the ribbon into a bow and glue it at the upper center of the largest heart.

Gifts from the groom to his groomsmen might include a writing portfolio, grooming set, paperweight, book with a leather book cover, key chain, gift certificate, bottle of fine wine in a bottle bag, or anything monogrammed.

Monogrammed Bottle Bag

The men in the wedding party will appreciate receiving a nice bottle of wine even more when it's presented in a distinctive *Ultrasuede* bag. The bag is especially simple because it needs no edge-finishing. (Fig. 4-23)

Fig. 4-23

MATERIALS NEEDED FOR EACH BAG

One 7" by 28" rectangle and one 1" by 28" strip of *Ultrasuede*

HOW-TOS

1. Use your computerized sewing machine or your needlework skills to embroider a monogram on each bag. Center the appropriate initials on the right side of the rectangle approximately 10" down from one short end.

2. Fold the narrow tie strip wrong sides together lengthwise and edge-stitch.

3. Fold the larger rectangle in half crosswise with wrong sides together, matching the bag's side edges.

4. Place the center point of the tie strip 3" from the upper edge, over the righthand side of the bag. (Fig. 4-24)

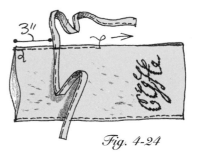

Fig. 4-24

5. Edge-stitch both side edges, seaming them together and catching the tie in the stitching.

CHAPTER FIVE
The Beautiful Bride

Much of the attention at any wedding is focused on the bride—it's her time to be a shining star! And when everyone looks at the bride, no doubt the first thing they'll notice is her gown.

Choosing the right gown can be a great challenge for any bride, because the options are practically unlimited and many dresses are very costly as well. The gown selected must suit the bride's personal style, fit her perfectly, and be as exquisitely flattering as possible.

Some brides have dreamed about and planned their special wedding dress for years, while others may have no idea what they are looking for. This chapter will answer many questions, even for those who are sure of the "exact" gown they want. In Chapter 6, we'll go on to discuss all of the accessories needed to complete the wedding ensemble, including headpieces and veils.

Selecting the Best Gown

The wedding dress must not only complement the bride, but it must also be in keeping with the wedding you've planned. The color, fabric, design, and overall style of the gown are all important considerations.

Style choices

The style of wedding you decide upon (see page 3) will have a direct effect on the gown you choose. Keep in mind these general guidelines:

FORMALITY—

Choose a dress appropriate for the formality (and time of day) of the wedding. (Fig. 5-1)

Formal
- White, off-white, or ivory
- Formal fabric, such as satin, taffeta, and lace
- A train—sweep or chapel length

Fig. 5-1

- Full-length, shoulder-length, or fingertip veil
- Attendants also wear formal dresses

Semiformal
- White, ivory, or pastel color
- Fabric such as linen, faille, and shantung
- Floor-length or tea-length
- Veil is elbow length or shorter

Informal
- White, pastel, or any color but black
- Fabric such as cotton, linen, and lace
- Long or calf-length (could be a suit)
- Short veil or headpiece is optional

A second marriage—For a second marriage, you may properly have a full-scale formal wedding, although informal and semiformal are more common. Any style worn by the second-time bride is appropriate, but without the veil and train. The wedding dress usually has less embellishment but can be elegant and sophisticated with laces, bows, and simple trims.

THEME—

The dress should be appropriate for any theme you may have chosen for the wedding. For example, if the event will have a country, modern and sophisticated, or Victorian feel, the gown can help establish the theme.

> ❝*My parents bought my first wedding dress at Lord & Taylor. When I was married the second time, I wanted to sew a dress with a Western theme. On vacation in Vail, Colorado, I found a perfect pattern in the fabric department at a Wal-Mart store. I had planned to search for light blue denim in Denver, and there was the exact fabric I was looking for at five dollars a yard! So my new Wal-Mart wedding dress has something old added—a yoke cut out of an antique linen tea towel that was cross-stitched with light blue deer. (I also used blue and white check piping and antique mother-of-pearl buttons.) One of my best friends, Marinda Stewart, hot-glued a headband for me and lent me a veil attached to a hair comb (the borrowed part of the outfit).*❞
>
> *Ann Boyce*
> Appliqué the Ann Boyce Way

SEASON—

Bridal professionals recognize two seasons—spring/summer and fall/winter. The type of fabric and style of the gown should be comfortable and appropriate for the time of year. Lighter-weight fabric and simpler designs are more suitable for spring and summer. (Fig. 5-2) Heavier fabrics, such as brocades or velvets, as well as more elaborate trims and high necklines, are appropriate for fall and winter. (See page 70 for more information on appropriate fabrics for the gown.)

SPRING/SUMMER FALL/WINTER

Fig. 5-2

Budget Helper

Don't forget the wedding budget when selecting a gown. Keep in mind the maximum that you can spend. The wedding dress may be very important to the entire occasion, but there are many other expenses to be considered.

Color considerations

There are no hard and fast rules for selecting a wedding gown color. Personal preference, the wedding formality, lighting, and the hour of the ceremony are all factors. Several options are available:

🐾 White is still the most popular color and can vary from a warm, creamy white to a cool, blue-white. If you prefer a white dress, try on both shades to decide which is most flattering to your skin tone and hair color.

🐾 Off-white and ivory are also favorites but are slightly more expensive. They can vary from light to deep tones.

🐾 Many dresses are also available with just a blush of color or in soft pastels. Another option is to wear white lace over a pastel underlining. These colors may be worn by a first-time bride as well as for a second marriage.

🐾 For an informal wedding, any flattering color can be selected. Also look for interesting color combinations in tints, hues, and shades of your favorite colors.

If you prefer just a touch of color with a white or ivory bridal ensemble, use colored flowers in the bridal bouquet or colored ribbons in the bouquet or headpiece.

Dress design

The wedding gown should help the bride look her most beautiful. Although many brides choose classic silhouettes, any dress design is acceptable as long as it suits the occasion and reflects a style becoming to the bride's height, weight, and personality. Consider comfort as well—perhaps the bride can choose a design she's felt good in before. To begin the selection process, look through bridal magazines to see which designs are popular and which ones you like most.

When selecting a design, the bride should first analyze her figure and height, then choose a design that accentuates her best features. It may be tempting to consider a dress with many elaborate features, but the design may be too overpowering, especially for a smaller figure. Look for balance, most often by accentuating the upper body and minimizing the lower.

CHOOSING FLATTERING FEATURES—

When selecting the dress design, consider each feature to determine whether it's flattering. (Fig. 5-3)

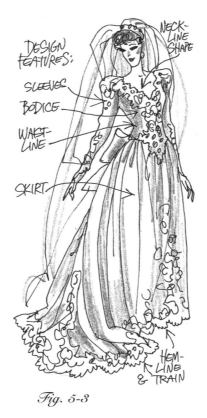

Fig. 5-3

Bodice—Vertical lines slenderize, so princess and A-line styles are slimming and flattering for most figure types. An elongated bodice or slightly dropped waistline creates the illusion of height and will de-emphasize the hips.

Neckline shape—Usually the first feature to be noticed, the neckline has a major influence on a striking design. The shape should flatter both the face and figure and be comfortable to wear. The neckline should not be too low or so high that it is constricting. High collars draw the eyes up; wide or off-the-shoulder necklines draw the eye outward and add width; low necklines are slimming and lengthen the torso.

Sleeves—The detail most linked to the season, sleeves add interest to the bodice and balance the lower half of the dress. Balloon, puffed, and ruffled sleeves add width to the upper body; dramatic long and full sleeves add vertical lines; long, straight sleeves camouflage both thin and heavy arms.

Waistline—A dress with a definite waistline will flatter most figure types. The Basque, a natural waistline in the back with a lower V-point in front, is the most popular and attractive for a variety of figures. It adds the illusion of height but still creates a waistline for taller and more slender figures. When the V-point is raised or lowered or added to the back waistline as well, the feature can be even more flattering for some.

Skirt—This gown feature is balanced and affected by all the other features. A full skirt helps to shape the waistline and camouflage the hips. Princess lines slenderize and add height; skirts pleated to the bodice will be more slenderizing than full gathers; a peplum added to the skirt will emphasize the hip area.

Hemline and train—These are both dictated by the formality of the wedding as well as by personal preference. Gowns are usually worn long or tea-length, unless the wedding is informal. Train lengths vary: a **sweep train** just brushes the floor and is the easiest to manage because there is no need for a bustle; a **chapel train** extends about a yard; and a **cathedral train** is longer than a yard. Both chapel and cathedral trains need to be bustled (see page 77), adding width and weight to the skirt. Trains are usually embellished to add weight so they'll hang more smoothly and neatly. A train can also be detachable so that it can be removed for the reception (also on page 77).

Gown back—Don't forget to give special attention to the back of the dress, too. It will be the feature seen most during the ceremony.

Other design details—Other factors that affect the overall appearance of the gown are fabric, laces, trims, and even tiny buttons. The entire look should be as flattering as possible to the bride.

COMPLEMENTARY SILHOUETTES—
Embellishments and trims can be added to the dress to draw attention to the wearer's best features, but avoid the tendency to overtrim. Keep in mind that ruffles and bows will add width and also can be overwhelming for a petite figure. Consider figure characteristics when selecting the most flattering silhouette:

Petite (Fig. 5-4)

Lengthen the look with princess or vertical lines.
- Avoid high necklines.
- Avoid full sleeves—fitted and cap sleeves give the illusion of height.
- Choose a natural or slightly raised waistline.
- Choose a moderate amount of trim—frills can be overwhelming.

PETITE:

Fig. 5-4

SHORT & FULL-FIGURED:

Fig. 5-5

- Avoid ruffles and tiers on skirts and also long trains—a chapel length train is best.
- Opt for delicate laces and avoid large patterns on both laces and fabric.
- Avoid weighty and heavily textured fabrics.

Short and full-figured (Fig. 5-5)
- Select a plain, simply styled gown.
- Look for vertical lines in the bodice and skirt.
- Pick a simple V-neckline.
- Choose a natural or slightly dropped waist.
- Choose a soft, flowing skirt.
- Avoid clingy fabric and ruffles.

Tall and slender (Fig. 5-6)
- Use detailing on either the upper or lower sections, but not on both.
- Look for a wide neckline (with gathers or ruffles, if desired).
- Select elaborate or off-the-shoulder sleeves.
- Choose horizontal pleats or detailing on the bodice.
- Pick a full or tiered skirt.
- A full train, ruffles and bows, or heavily textured fabric can be worn.

TALL & SLENDER:

Fig. 5-6

Full-busted (Fig. 5-8)

- Choose a V-neckline with no ruffles or bows.
- Select simple sleeves with no off-the-shoulder styling.
- Choose an elongated bodice.
- Princess lines will be flattering.
- Add elongated appliqué trim.
- Look for a full, embellished skirt.

Small-busted (Fig. 5-9)

- Avoid V-necklines.
- Add a ruffle to the neckline.
- Look for an embellished bodice.

Heavy arms (Fig. 5-10)

- Choose a sweetheart or other interesting neckline.
- Select simple elbow- or wrist-length sleeves or tapered leg-of-mutton sleeves and avoid cap sleeves.
- Avoid an off-the-shoulder or strapless design.
- Look for vertical skirt lines.
- Add skirt interest with a peplum, bustle, or gathers.

Tall and full-figured (Fig. 5-7)

- Opt for simple tailoring.
- Choose a V-neckline.
- Avoid voluminous ruffles.
- Avoid body-hugging fabric.

Full hips (Fig. 5-11)

- Accentuate the upper body with big sleeves or an off-the-shoulder style.

- Choose an embellished and elongated bodice with minimal skirt interest.
- Look for pleats instead of gathers on the upper skirt.
- Select a bias-cut skirt and non-clingy fabrics.
- Avoid large bows at the back.

Curvaceous body (Fig. 5-12)

- Select plain, simple lines with equal interest on the upper and lower dress.
- Choose a deep, open neckline.
- Pick a lightly embellished bodice.

Fig. 5-12

- Look for an off-the-shoulder style.
- Choose a natural or slightly dropped waistline.

Smart Shopping

After you have an idea of the type of gown you'll be looking for, you must decide where to find it. Your options are to buy, borrow, rent, hire a dressmaker, make it yourself, or use any combination of these.

Designer gowns start at about $1,500, while the average cost of a wedding dress is about $800. The more intricate the trim and hand-sewing, the more expensive the dress will be. The type of fabric and lace will also contribute to the cost of the dress, with silk and imported laces used in the most expensive gowns.

Three-quarters of all brides buy their dresses, so there is a wide selection available. However, you must shop early because some stores may have a six-week or longer delivery time, depending on their suppliers and the season. Most dresses will need some alterations, too, so allow for that in your schedule. Don't buy too soon, though, because your size and taste may change and fashion trends can vary.

Shopping tips

A wide variety of styles are available with different fabrics, quality, and pricing. When shopping for a gown:

- Begin early. Allow time to shop at different stores and for trying on many gowns.

- Bring only one person with you when shopping. It's better to have only the opinion of one person who will be honest with you. Ignore the flattery of an overzealous salesperson who is anxious for a sale.

- Check for spacious and clean dressing rooms.

- The dresses available for trying on should be clean and unwrinkled.

- Inform the bridal shop of the amount you've budgeted for a dress or give them a price range you've determined. Then stick to the limit you've set.

- Take pictures of your favorite design features with you, as well as pictures of accessories. But also keep an open mind to other suggestions.

🌸 Wear suitable undergarments and shoes for trying on dresses.

🌸 Wear your hair in a style similar to how you will wear it for the wedding. Hairstyle will make a difference on the neckline you choose.

🌸 When trying on the dresses, ask yourself:

Fig. 5-13

1. Is the style one that I like?

2. Is it comfortable to wear?

3. Can I sit, stand, and dance in it easily?

4. Will it be easy to get in and out of a car?

5. Is it the quality I prefer?

6. If it has a long train, is it easy to bustle?

🌸 Allow enough time at each shop for trying on dresses.

Budget Helper

When ordering a dress, you may want to make some changes in styling, color, laces, and fabric. Trims can be added or removed and a different sleeve or neckline can be chosen. Remember that all changes will cost extra and need to be considered as part of the dress budget. Also note that bridal sizes don't compare to other dress sizing, so order by your measurements and watch out for a shop that orders dresses too large and expects you to pay for expensive alterations.

🌸 Understand all store terms and policies before you put down a deposit and ask the following questions:

1. How long will it take to get the dress?

2. What is the payment policy? The deposit required? Refund policy? Cancellation policy? Credit-card protection?

3. What is the estimate for alterations? Get a written estimate before starting the alterations.

4. What free services are offered? Pressing or steaming the dress?

5. What else is included in the price of the gown?

🌸 When ordering, get a receipt that includes the price, color, size, style number, promised delivery date, and any special order requests. Keep every receipt in your planning notebook.

Where to look

Many brides begin their gown search at bridal shops. There are a number of other available alternatives, however, so consider each one before making your final selection. If you purchase a dress from a discounted source, remember that the price usually will not include the full services offered by a bridal shop, department store, or personal dressmaker. Solicit recommendations from friends, attend bridal shows, and refer to bridal magazines to help choose your source.

BRIDAL SHOPS—

Buying from a full-retail bridal shop can be the most expensive option, or you might find a great buy. Quality, sizing, style, and price will vary with the shop. When buying from a full-retail bridal store, you are also paying for service, assistance, and attention to small details. A reputable store will make right any mistake in fitting, alteration, and sizing. But buying at a full-service shop also means paying full price for the dress unless you're buying a sample or sale garment.

SIMPLE EVENING DRESS

EMBELLISHED FOR THE WEDDING

Fig. 5-14

DEPARTMENT STORES—

Many department stores have a bridal salon that functions much like an independent bridal shop. However, if the store does not carry bridal wear and you're looking for a nontraditional dress, the evening-wear department can be an excellent place to look—a dress can often be purchased at a budget price and embellishments added to individualize it. (Fig. 5-14) This practical approach leaves you free to remove the additions later and get much more use from the dress.

DISCOUNT STORES—

Dresses purchased from discount stores may be designer samples or discontinued styles with savings from 25 percent to 50 percent off retail. Services, such as fitting or alterations, will probably not be included in the price, and the dress usually has to be paid for in advance.

MAIL-ORDER SOURCES—

Wedding dresses can be purchased by mail-order at a price lower than full retail, but you'll be purchasing sight unseen. No fitting or alteration is included, so these costs will be an added expense and you'll need to find a reputable dressmaker to help you. In some cases, you also may have a problem returning the dress if it doesn't meet your specifications.

CONSIGNMENT SHOPS—

The gowns available at consignment shops have usually been sold by brides after a wedding and can be excellent bargains. Alterations and repairs are not included, so check the condition of the dress carefully. The purchase is final, so make certain the style is one you really prefer.

CLASSIFIED ADS—

Check your local newspaper for good buys on gowns. The dress may be offered by a bride after the wedding or it even may be in perfect condition if the wedding was canceled or postponed. In most cases, the seller needs the cash, so there is some bargaining room, even though the offered price may be 50 percent or more off retail. Plan to pay extra for repairs or alterations, if they're needed.

RENTING—

Renting wedding attire is generally acceptable, most often for the men in the wedding party. Wedding gowns may also be rented from a formal-wear shop. Prices range from $75 to $600 for a dress that would retail for $1,000 to $2,000. The dresses are professionally dry-cleaned and may include minor alterations, but rental may not be the best choice if major alterations need to be made. Rentals usually require a $100 deposit.

BORROWING—

Consider borrowing a dress from a friend or family member, especially if you want to wear a family heirloom. Be certain, though, that it's a dress you really like. (You may want to have it dry-cleaned first to make sure it is suitable for you.) When borrowing from a friend, etiquette dictates that she has already been married for one year.

There is also a limit to the amount of alterations that can be made on a borrowed gown. After the dress is worn, the alterations should be removed and the dress dry-cleaned before it is returned. When altering, be sure that large stitches are used to avoid leaving any permanent marks on the fabric.

A sentimental choice may be to wear the mother's wedding dress or another vintage garment. In this case, the only cost may be for alterations. The gown may be reused intact or combined with new fabric into a new style. Try on the dress and then get an estimate for any remodeling or restoration. (See Restoring a Vintage Dress on page 78.)

CUSTOM DRESSMAKING—

Whether you're making your own dress or having it made by a professional dressmaker, you can get the exact dress you have in mind. (See Custom Sewing on page 69.) Dressmaking is also the best option if you can't find what you want from any other source. It doesn't hurt to look at retail first, though, if only for ideas.

What to look for

Whether purchasing the dress or having it made, look for quality of workmanship and fit:

🍂 Is the dress finished as well on the inside as it is on the outside?

🍂 Are the seamlines neat and straight with no outline of the seam allowance showing on the right side?

🍂 Are the seams on the dress layers sewn separately so that the dress hangs neatly?

🍂 Is the dress lined so that undergarments don't show through and the garment holds its shape?

🍂 Is the interfacing correctly used so that it does not show from the right side?

🍂 Is the beading secure with no beads missing?

🍂 Are the lace motifs balanced?

🍂 Are the hooks, loops, and buttons securely attached?

🍂 Is the garment clean and pressed?

🍂 Does the dress flatter the figure?

🍂 Is the dress comfortable to wear?

Custom Fitting

Taking measurements

There is no sizing standard for purchased bridal dresses, so it's important to take measurements and select the size according to them.

Use accurate measurements because wedding dresses are close-fitting. Insist on measuring over the undergarments that will be worn for the wedding, using a vinyl tape measure (a cloth tape will stretch). Take bust, waist, hip, and length measurements (wearing shoes with the same heel height being worn for the wedding), including one from the base of the throat to the hemline, one from the bone at the back neckline to the natural waistline, and one from the shoulder bone to the wrist bone with the elbow slightly bent (for the sleeve length). (Fig. 5-15)

Ask to see the manufacturer's sizing chart and order the size that matches your largest measurement. The other areas can always be altered by taking them in, but it's much more difficult to let out part of the dress. Be sure that the size you've ordered is marked on the sales receipt.

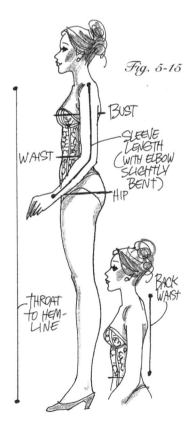

Fig. 5-15

BUST

SLEEVE LENGTH (WITH ELBOW SLIGHTLY BENT)

WAIST

HIP

THROAT TO HEM- LINE

BACK WAIST

Alterations

Alterations may need to be made on the gown if it is purchased, borrowed, or rented. Approximately 60 percent of the time, gowns will require some custom fitting because they're usually body-hugging and are made to standard measurements.

Alterations might include fitting the bodice, shortening or lengthening the skirt, and adjusting the waistline. Be sure to wear the correct undergarments and shoes during fitting. The dress can feel quite different from any other one worn in the past—it will probably be heavier, have time-consuming closures, and may require a petticoat.

The majority of alterations involve adjusting the length of the gown. If there is decorative trim around the hemline, length alterations are usually made at the waistline seam. The length should be measured while standing on a hard floor.

If there is no waistline seam or if waistline alterations are not possible, the trim must be carefully removed—it may be just basted or tacked on loosely. The new hemline can be finished with narrow balanced serging or a narrow top-stitched hem. Then the trim is lapped and top-stitched over the edge, using a single or double-galloon lace for a scalloped hem. (Fig. 5-16)

Fig. 5-16

If you select a dressmaker to do the alterations, do some preliminary checking:

- Ask for recommendations from previous clients.

- Look at examples of past work.

- Confirm the level and length of experience.

- Insist on the best alterations that money can buy. Two or three fittings may be necessary, with the final fitting close to the wedding day.

Even minor alterations may involve taking the dress and the lining apart. Check for the following results after custom-fitting and alterations:

- Make sure beads are not caught or sewn into the seams.

- The bodice should fit snugly and smoothly with no wrinkles.

- The length of the dress should be 3/4" to 1" above the floor when wearing a petticoat.

- The petticoat or slip should be 1/2" to 1" shorter than the dress hemline edge.

- If the dress has a bustle, check the appearance. Does it look as well bustled as unbustled?

- Any lace scallops should be maintained and not turned under.

- All fastenings, such as hooks and eyes, should be secure.

- The dress should be clean and well pressed or steamed.

Custom Sewing

Many brides choose to have their dress custom-designed and sewn so that it will reflect their personal style and be their own special creation. Every detail can be made exactly to specifications—you can even copy a designer original. Another advantage to having a gown sewn is that there are no costly alterations—it's already made to fit.

When determining who will sew the dress, remember that the job will require more ability and expertise than sewing most other outfits. Whether you sew your own dress depends on your sewing skill level and your time. Even if you have the ability and will save money, the job may be too stressful at a time when you'll have many other pressures.

Finding a dressmaker

If you choose to have the dress sewn by a dressmaker, remember that you are still the designer and you can make the design decisions. To find a dressmaker, ask for recommendations from fabric stores, friends, and dry cleaners. Ask for and check the references you are given. Make sure the dressmaker is willing to take the time to consult on every detail. Check on these specifics:

📎 Show clippings of the design details you have selected. Is she (or he) able to sew this style, especially if it means combining patterns?

📎 Talk about the fabric you prefer. Has she enough experience and is she comfortable sewing with this fabric? Or will the type of fabric have to be changed because of her expertise?

📎 Does she have suggestions for a better choice of pattern and fabric?

📎 Who will purchase the fabric, trims, and any other notions? Can either of you buy fabric at wholesale prices?

📎 Ask to see samples of her work. Check the hems—is the stitching invisible? Check the zipper and other finishing details. Is the inside of the dress finished well?

📎 Check references. Was her work delivered on time?

📎 Decide on beading, pearls, trim, lace, and embroidery.

📎 Ask her price range for sewing this design and discuss payment of the fee. Usually half is due at the first fitting and the balance on completion of the dress.

A good dressmaker ensures a good fit. Three to four fittings are usually needed during the construction process: pattern fitting (Fig. 5-17); muslin fitting; bodice fitting (with it basted together); and final fitting, one to two weeks before the wedding.

Fig. 5-17

If either you or a dressmaker are sewing the dress, allow ample time, sometimes as much as six months before the wedding, for ordering fabric and trim, as well as for fitting.

Selecting a pattern

All major pattern companies have excellent wedding dress patterns. If necessary, combine design details from two or more different patterns from the same company:

📎 Don't hesitate to use almost any type of pattern as long as the fabric is appropriate.

📎 Check the pattern book's dress and lingerie sections for unusual options, including sleeve, hemline, and trim treatments.

🍃 Consider using a simple design and enhancing it with beading, appliqués, laces, and trims.

🍃 Choose the design for the bridal dress first, then use a similar design for the bridesmaids' dresses.

🍃 For the easiest fitting, select a princess-line design. Then buy the pattern by the upper body measurement.

Choosing the fabric

The most traditional fabrics for wedding dresses are satins and taffetas in various fibers, such as acetate, polyester, and silk, in a wide range of weights and finishes. Acetate is a weaker fabric, the least expensive, and will waterspot easily. Silk is the most expensive, but it may also waterspot. The most popular, affordable, and widely available fabrics include:

LACE—

A classic wedding fabric that adds a rich, opulent, and romantic look to the wedding dress. It is available in a variety of widths, from 36" to 60", and can be cut apart for lace motifs. It is generally more economical to cut motifs from lace yardage than it is to buy them.

Imported laces are the most expensive and are 36" wide in 4- to 6-yard lengths. Many, such as imported Alençon lace, have a hand-worked design. Alençon is reembroidered with cord for a slightly raised effect and its motifs make an attractive embellishment appliqué, too. (Fig. 5-18)

Fig. 5-18

Position a lace appliqué near the face as an attractive focus. Use narrower lace for a portion of the dress, for example, the trim on an heirloom look or a peplum. Domestic laces, like the widely used Chantilly lace, are wider and can be used for larger sections or for the entire dress. Most domestic laces are 45" to 60" wide and can accommodate larger pattern pieces. Take advantage of the scalloped edges on some laces, using them as hem edges or lapping them over seams.

Before purchasing lace, place it over the fabric to make sure it gives the look you want. On larger-patterned laces, it's important to balance the motifs and match them at the seamlines. The smaller the lace design, the less you'll need to match.

SATIN—

A smooth, lustrous fabric that accents the body curves. It varies in weight and types and can be used any time of day or year. A popular type of satin is peau de soie, which is not as drapable as other satins.

TAFFETA—

A crisp, smooth fabric, also available in varying weights. It is appropriate for bouffant details, such as full skirts, bows, and sleeves, but is not a good choice for drapable designs. For more surface design and texture, consider moiré taffeta.

BROCADE—

A dramatic, heavier-weight fabric with pattern and dimension. Either or both sides of this tapestry-like fabric may be used as the right side of the fabric. Select brocade for a more tailored gown, a straight skirt, or a suit.

FAILLE AND TISSUE FAILLE—

Finely ribbed fabrics that are opaque and lustrous. They're available in varying weights, with tissue faille being the lighter.

VELVETS AND VELVETEENS—

Rich, plush fabrics, usually used during the fall and winter. Use velvet for a drapable design and velveteen, a stiffer fabric, for a more structured garment.

SHEERS—

Including organza, georgette, and chiffon. Use them over other fabrics in bodices and skirts or for full gathered skirts and full sleeves. They can also be used with lace as an underlining. These fabrics may take more expertise to sew but are easily finished with a serged rolled-edge hem.

COTTONS—

Including voile, eyelet, dotted swiss, batiste, and lawn. They can be either soft or crisp and are usually used for semiformal and informal summer weddings.

SILKS—

Including taffeta, charmeuse, chiffon, faille, crepe de chine, broadcloth, brocade, peau de soie, and organza. Available as pure fibers or blends, these fabrics hang gracefully and are found in the most expensive dresses.

Most fabric stores have everything you'll need to make a wedding dress or are willing to order it for you. Check the dress silhouette to determine what fabric to use. For a more structured style, a firmer fabric, such as brocade, will be required. A very full skirt needs a drapable fabric. Follow the fabric selection recommendations on the back of the pattern envelope as a guide. (Fig. 5-19) If you are not familiar with fabrics or trims, ask the sales clerk for help or refer to *Claire Shaeffer's Fabric Sewing Guide*.

Fig. 5-19

Compare the yardage requirement with the cost of the fabric. If lots of fabric is required, you may want to use less expensive fabric and lace for the dress and add trims, beading, and more expensive lace to embellish it.

Lining, underlining, and interfacing

Lining the dress gives shape and body to the gown, prevents stretching, and reduces wrinkling. It is also important for covering uncomfortable seam allowances, caused by netting, sequins, or other scratchy materials. Lining also protects and covers the inner construction of the dress. If lining pieces are not included in the pattern, they can be cut from the garment pattern pieces. Often the bodice and skirt are lined, eliminating the need for a slip. Choose a matching lining fabric, such as lightweight polyester, acetate, or batiste, that is a lighter weight than the outer fabric.

Most garments will require a lightweight underlining for garment support and body. An underlining is also a lighter weight than the outer fabric, often a batiste, voile, nylon net, or organza. A sew-in interfacing may be used for underlining as well as garment support, especially when sewing heavier trim to the dress.

Interfacing is seldom needed in a wedding dress, especially if it's underlined, supported with elastics and boning, and/or lined. However, a nylon net such as crinoline can be used to add body and crispness to bows, collars, cuffs, and other details without adding weight. Crinoline also can be used for sleeve headers and ruffles on underslips. Cool-fuse interfacing can be used for lighter-weight fabrics that are not crushable when pressed. Avoid fused interfacings for beaded, sequined, and velvet-type fabrics.

Making a fitting muslin

When using special-occasion fabric (and because a wedding dress is a close-fitting garment), it is advisable to make a sample garment for fitting before cutting into the more expensive fabric. Use muslin or an old sheet for the fitting garment. You may need to try several patterns before achieving the desired look and fit.

If the dress has a waistline seam, only the bodice (and perhaps the sleeves) needs to be fitted. The focus will be on the upper body, requiring more complicated fitting than that of the waist or hip area.

Be sure to allow for underlining and lining during fitting. Both of these, as well as boning and stays, give shape to a fitted bodice. It should fit perfectly— like a glove. Elastic helps in fitting an off-the-shoulder style, anchoring the garment to the body. When fitting, be sure to allow for the drape of the fabric and make sure tightened elastic doesn't restrict arm movement.

Constructing the gown

While constructing and fitting the wedding dress, keep the floor dirt-free by laying clean sheets under the sewing and pressing areas. Wash your hands before starting to sew and before fitting. Additional tips for construction include:

🙠 For ease in cutting slippery special-occasion fabric, cover the cutting surface with a flannel-backed vinyl tablecloth. Place the flannel side up to keep the fabric from slipping.

🙠 Pin carefully, within the seam allowances if possible, to avoid marking the fabric. When pinning loosely woven fabrics, use large-headed pins or small safety pins.

🙠 On off-the-shoulder dresses, use boning to help with fitting and inner support and to stiffen, mold, and maintain the bodice shape. Covered boning is lightweight and doesn't require a separate casing—simply glue-baste and then top-stitch along both sides of the covering fabric, using a zipper foot.

For more in-depth information on sewing and serging techniques, refer to *A Step-by-Step Guide to Your Sewing Machine* and *Serged Garments in Minutes*.

Selecting the closings

Loops and tiny buttons are the traditional closings for the back and sleeves of a wedding gown. On more expensive dresses and for more durability, an invisible or light coil zipper is used on the back, along with the buttons and loops. When an invisible zipper is closed, no stitching shows on the right side of the garment. (Fig. 5-20)

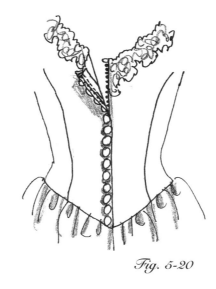

Fig. 5-20

Button loops can be made from bias strips of the dress fabric, but the task can be time-consuming and requires precision in stitching and trimming. Loop trim, as well as elastic loop trim, can be purchased by the yard, but usually only in white. (It can be dyed to match any other dress color.) For off-white or ivory dresses, dye loop trim by steeping it in a pot or pan of strong tea until it reaches the desired shade.

To save time, purchase buttons already covered or use pearl half-buttons. If you're covering buttons, lightly dampen the fabric before covering them (but be sure to test first for water spotting). The fabric will shrink tightly around the button when it dries. For ease in buttoning, begin from the bottom and button upward.

Proper pressing

When pressing, use a good iron and clean ironing board. To avoid water spotting and delustering of sequins or beading, press with a dry iron. Press seam allowances open using the point of the iron (or press over a seam roll) to prevent the seam allowances from showing on the right side. Press lace right side down using a press cloth, to prevent crushing it or catching the iron in the lace openings.

Special Detailing

Whether your gown will be one of simple elegance or the ultimate in embellishment, frosted with beads, pearls, and lace, special detailing adds greatly to the overall look. Check wedding magazines for ideas or take the dress to a professional dressmaker and ask for suggestions.

Trimming the gown

A wide array of ornamental trims, from simple to elaborate, is available to decorate any wedding dress, both purchased and custom-sewn. (Fig. 5-21) It's often difficult to decide which trim and application to use with the variety of lace trim, beadwork, sequins, ribbon, appliqués, ruffles, bows and rosettes, piping, embroidery, covered buttons, and looped buttonholes at hand. Prices vary widely as well.

Fig. 5-21

Bejeweled wedding gowns used to be a symbol of the wealth of the bride's family, but today most gowns are embellished with several types of trim. A rule of thumb is to add a trim when the gown fits perfectly but something seems to be missing. Trim is used to define and accent specific areas of the gown, especially those areas to which you want to draw the eye.

Budget Helper

You may choose to select a simple bridal gown and embellish it with your own design, but keep in mind that all the trims should be dry-cleanable. Some, especially beading, dull and disintegrate when exposed to drycleaning fluids.

Trims, such as piping or pearl strands, can be sewn into the seamlines of collars, necklines, waistlines, and cuffs. Bands highlighted with sequins, beads, and pearls are often used to outline the edges of necklines, sleeves, and lower hems. Pearls, sequins, and other beading are used to embellish fabric, trace lace designs, and layer over other trims, such as ribbons or lace appliqués.

LACE TRIM—

Available both flat and gathered in widths of ¼" to 6" and wider, some lace trims have scallops, called *galloons*, on both edges and some have one or two straight edges, which are easier to gather or insert into a seam. Quickly make gathered trim from flat lace using the differential feed on a serger—adjust to the highest positive differential-feed setting and, with a long stitch, serge over the straight edge of the lace. It will gather as you sew.

Lace yardage can be cut apart and also used as trim on garment areas such as necklines, waistlines, sleeves, and hems. Shape the lace by laying it over the garment and steaming to curve it into position. Top-stitch the lace to the fabric using a long, narrow zigzag. For highly curved areas, clip the lace between the motifs and lap it slightly to fit. Then top-stitch to secure. (Fig. 5-22)

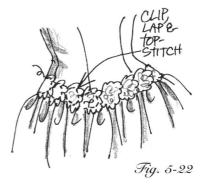

Fig. 5-22

When purchasing finished lace trim, allow ⅓ to ½ yard extra for shaping, matching, and raveling. After cutting, before applying the lace, seal loose ends with masking tape if they have a tendency to ravel. Determine lace trim placement before seaming or hemming. Finish with a narrow hem or serging, then top-stitch, zigzag, or hand-stitch the trim over the finished edge (see Fig. 5-16).

BANDED TRIMS—

Strips of beads, lace, or combinations of both are used to trim edges and cover seams, such as the waistline. To easily apply a band, first glue-baste it in place using a glue stick. Allow the glue to dry, then top-stitch along the long edges, sewing in the same direction on both sides. (Fig. 5-23)

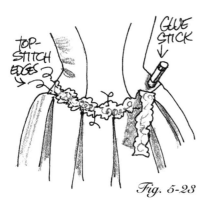

Fig. 5-23

RUFFLES AND RUCHING—

In addition to being used in the wedding dress, the fabric you select can be cut into strips, gathered for ruffles or ruching, and used to trim the neckline, sleeves, and/or hem:

1. Cut a strip the desired ruffle depth plus ½" by twice the length of the area to be trimmed. (Fig. 5-24)

2. Finish all four edges of the ruffle strip with a narrow ⅛" hem folded twice to the wrong side and top-stitched (or serge-finish them with a rolled-edge hem).

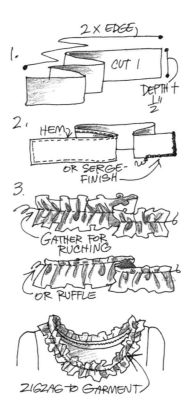

Fig. 5-24

3. Gather through the center of the strip for ruching or along one edge for a ruffle. Pull up the gathering stitches to fit, then top-stitch the ruffle to the fabric by zigzagging with a long, narrow stitch on top of the gathering stitches.

APPLIQUÉS—

Use purchased or custom-made appliqués, usually of lace, beading, or a combination of both, to enhance any wedding ensemble. They work equally well on simple suits and dresses, elaborate gowns, and bridal accessories.

Feature lace appliqués on the bodice, sleeves, or skirt. You may choose to purchase them or cut them from lace yardage, using small sharp scissors and leaving a narrow strip of netting around

each motif. When determining the placement of an appliqué, balance the lace motifs on the center front or back of the dress.

When applying appliqués to a skirt and train, pin them on for placement but complete the hemming before sewing them onto the fabric. (Fig. 5-25) If the train will be bustled, be sure any appliqués will be visible then, too, before sewing them on permanently.

Fig. 5-25

Choose one of several methods for applying appliqués, depending upon the type. Because many appliqués are sensitive to heat and can melt, lose their sheen, and scorch with pressing or dissolve during dry-cleaning, you may need to select an application method that allows them to be easily removed and reapplied. Application options include:

◦ Hand-sewing in place with matching thread.

◦ Gluing with a dry-cleanable glue, such as Delta's *Jewel Glue* or Bond's *Victory Fabric Glue*. (Always test first. Dry-cleaning solvents not only can dissolve some glues but will disintegrate some types of pearls and other ornamentation as well.)

◦ Attaching with a safety pin from the wrong side.

◦ Fusing the appliqué to the dress (but be sure to test first to see if steaming and fusing will work on both the fabric and the appliqué):

1. Cut paper-backed fusible web ⅛" smaller than the appliqué or in smaller sections and fuse it to the wrong side.

2. Remove the paper and fuse the appliqué in place on the right side of the fabric, using a press cloth and steaming well.

◦ Top-stitching with a straight-stitch or narrow zigzag. For a see-through effect, carefully trim the fabric ⅛" from the stitching on the underside of a lace appliqué.

BEADING—

Beading can be added to any area of the gown, but most often it is applied over lace. (Fig. 5-26) Place the beadwork where it will be the most visible, using a color and size appropriate for the fabric and dress style.

For ease of application, attach beads before construction—smaller garment sections are much eas-

Fig. 5-26

ier to handle. The beading will usually follow the lace design, but, in some cases, you might want to bead following your own unique design. To draw a beading design on the fabric:

1. Trace the design onto a piece of lightweight tear-away stabilizer, slightly larger than the design. (Fig. 5-27)

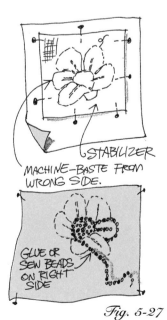

STABILIZER
MACHINE-BASTE FROM WRONG SIDE.

GLUE OR SEW BEADS ON RIGHT SIDE

Fig. 5-27

2. Place the stabilizer on the wrong side of the fabric with the design up.

3. Using matching thread in the bobbin, machine-baste over the design lines.

4. Attach the beads along the stitching line on the right side of the fabric.

Beading is usually applied by hand—either sewn onto finer-quality dresses or glued onto less expensive ones. When applying beads by hand-sewing, use matching all-purpose thread and small, loose stitches. A simple alternative to individual hand-beading is to purchase beading by the yard and sew it on with hand-stitching or by top-stitching using a zigzag, a special presser foot, and matching or monofilament nylon thread. You may also choose to serge beads to the fabric, using a rolled-edge or flatlock stitch.

When gluing beads to the fabric, use a dry-cleanable glue (see those recommended under Appliqués, above) and remember to test first. The glue should dry clear and hold up through multiple drycleanings. When gluing:

1. Place layers of tissue paper under the dress or dress sections.

2. Stretch the fabric taut and hold it in place with pattern weights.

3. Glue along the placement markings by first putting a dot of glue on the fabric and then, with tweezers, position-

ing the beads or beading. Allow for drying time before moving.

PIPING—

Custom-make beaded piping by serging or zigzagging pearls or beads to a bias-cut tricot strip such as *Seams Great*. Special beading feet are available for many models of both sergers and sewing machines. (On a serger, the beads must be small enough to fit between the needle and knife and rest in the foot's tunnel and for the upper looper to pass over them.) Use matching thread or lightweight monofilament nylon and a long rolled-edge stitch on a serger or use a long, narrow zigzag on a sewing machine. Slowly serge or sew over the beading, attaching it to the tricot. (Fig. 5-28)

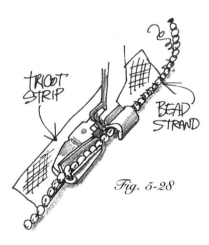

Fig. 5-28

Use the same technique for making satin piping on a bias-cut tricot strip. Serge or zigzag over several strands of matching filler, such as pearl cotton, using pearl rayon thread. Or use monofilament nylon thread over satin cording.

RIBBON—

Ribbon is a quick and easy trim to use because it's widely available in a variety of colors and widths, plus both edges are pre-finished. Apply ribbons, sewn flat, to outline the neckline and sleeves. They're also good on a belt or in hair ornaments. Ribbon roses and bows can be used as accents on the skirt, sleeves, or bodice, either alone or in combination with other trims. Also consider using satin ribbon for ruffled or pleated trim—the edge is already finished. Simply measure the area to be trimmed and cut the ribbon twice that length. Gather one edge of the ribbon for a ruffle or gather through the center of wider ribbon to create ruching. (See page 74 for instructions on ruching fabric strips.)

BOWS—

Bows can be made quickly and easily from either fabric or lace. They can be used to ornament the dress, often at the back waistline. (Fig. 5-29) Both bows and rosettes (see next page) can be used to set off the folds of a bustle and cover any hooks and loops needed to attach or fold up a train. A bow can be used as a simple headpiece, too.

One of the simplest bows is made by wrapping a tie around the center of a folded fabric circle. Cut the bow strip twice the width you want to make the finished bow plus ½". Cut another strip twice the width you want the tie:

1. Fold the bow strip lengthwise, right sides together, and sew the long cut edges together

Fig. 5-29

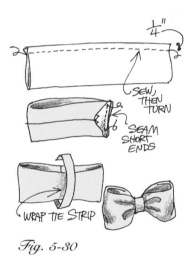

Fig. 5-30

using a ¼" seam allowance. (Fig. 5-30)

2. Turn the bow right side out and, matching the seamlines, seam the ends together as far as possible. Refold, centering the seam on the underside.

3. Fold the tie strip in half lengthwise and seam with right sides together. Turn the strip right side out and center the seam on the tie's under-

side. Wrap the tie around the center of the bow tightly and hand-sew the ends together.

To serge the bow instead of sewing it, fold both the bow and tie strips wrong sides together and serge-seam, using a ¼" allowance and centering both the seams to the underside—there's no need for turning. For a fancier bow, hand-sew a rosette (see below) over the bow center.

ROSETTES—

Fabric or ribbon folded or gathered in the shape of a rose is often used as an embellishment on wedding gowns and accessories. (See page 126 for instructions on making ribbon rosettes.)

Gathered fabric rosettes can be made any size, but the larger ones may need to be interfaced with crinoline and made from a longer fabric strip for a more pleasing fullness. Cut the rosette strip on the bias, if possible, for the prettiest drape, or cut on the crosswise grain as an alternative:

1. Cut a fabric strip 45" long by twice the desired petal width. (Fig. 5-31)

Fig. 5-31   2 × PETAL WIDTH

2. Fold the fabric in half lengthwise and gather the cut edges together by sewing or serging. Round the corners with the serger knives or before beginning to sew on a conventional machine.

3. Begin gathering tightly from one end, shaping the fabric into a rosette. Hand-sew the gathered edges together on the underside and attach the gathered area to the garment or accessory.

To make a removable rosette, cut two or three circles of crinoline or other stiff nylon net. Baste the circles together around the outer edges. Hand-sew the gathered rosette edges to the stacked net circles, then attach the netting to the area being decorated.

DETACHABLE TRAIN—

A detachable train of any length can be added to a floor-length gown or tied over a miniskirt. (Fig. 5-32) After the wedding, it can be removed

Fig. 5-32

before the reception to free the bride from the extra weight and fabric. This is especially desirable if she will be dancing. Attach the train with ties, hooks, or buttons at the waistline seam so that it can be removed easily.

Detachable trains are practical when the fabric is a delicate lace or has been reclaimed from an heirloom gown.

Bustling a train

If the train is not detachable, a wrist loop may be added so that the bride can hold it off the floor. Or the train can be folded up into an attractive bustle sometime after the wedding and before the reception. The bottom of the train should be about 1" off the floor for the easiest walking and dancing. Use one of the following bustling methods:

Fold the top of the skirt up and over the lifted train— This method is usually the most attractive and comfortable. (Fig. 5-33)

Fig. 5-33

1. Measure from the waistline seam to 1" above the floor.

2. Mark this measurement up from the center end of the train, pin-marking it on the skirt. (Fig. 5-34)

3. Raise the pin-mark to the center-back seamline, folding up the excess fabric at the top of the skirt (but not the lining), and pin it there.

4. On either side of the pin-mark, raise up the outer edges of the train and pin them in flattering spots on the sides of the back with the train edges 1" off the floor.

5. Raise and pin one or more places on either side, folding the train attractively, so the new bustled hemline is evenly off the floor.

6. Attach hooks and thread loops at the pinned positions, hid-

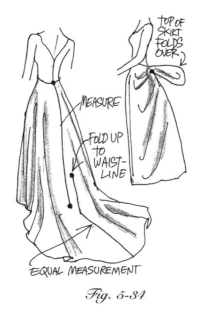

Fig. 5-34

ing them under appliqués, lace, or bows. Make sure the thread loops are secure by making them with two or three strands of strong thread.

Fold the train up and over the top of the skirt—This is the quickest bustling method. (Fig.

5-35) Follow the instructions for the bustling method above but raise and pin the skirt to the waistline seam on the *outside* of the dress. The folds need to be arranged attractively and equally because they will be featured at the back waistline.

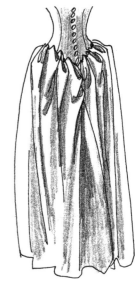

Fig. 5-35

Restoring a Vintage Dress

An older or "vintage" garment can be worn or used as part of the wedding dress even if the fabric is not perfect or if the dress is the wrong size. (Fig. 5-36) Inspect an older gown carefully:

🍂 How does it fit?

🍂 Does the style need to be changed?

🍂 Are there underarm stains that can be disguised or covered?

🍂 Can it be altered? How much alteration needs to be done and will it have to be done professionally?

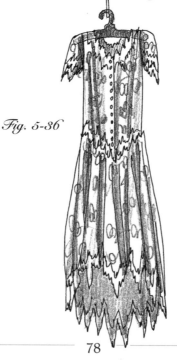

Fig. 5-36

🍂 Are the sleeves too tight and can they be removed?

🍂 Can embellishments be used to cover worn places?

If many changes need to be made, consider taking the dress to a restorer, who will clean and repair it. He (or she) can refit it and give you suggestions for refurbishing. Cotton fabric is the easiest to restore because it can be bleached and dyed. Taffeta and satin will never look new. Silk cannot be bleached and will not release stains.

A professional dressmaker can also do the restoration or, if you're an experienced seamstress, you may want to do it yourself. Before taking the dress apart, have it professionally dry-cleaned (but check with the dry cleaner first to see if they will be liable for any fabric deterioration during cleaning). If any part of the dress, such as the collar or the lace around the skirt, has deteriorated, you can replace it or modify the dress style. Consider these restoration techniques:

🖎 If the bodice and underarm are frayed, open the seams and line the underside of the dress with lightweight fusible interfacing. Or, if the fabric cannot be ironed, sew in a batiste underlining color-matched to the dress.

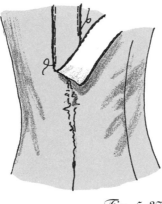

Fig. 5-37

🖎 If the fabric has deteriorated and is in shreds, find a matching type and color of fabric—natural fabric works best. Cut the new fabric into strips, finish them with a serged rolled edge or a narrow hand-stitched hem, and hand- or machine-stitch the strips in place over the shredded areas. (Fig. 5-37) Apply decorative trim over new fabric strips to disguise the refurbishing.

🖎 If the restoration fabric is not a close color match, you may have to dye it. Dip it into strong tea several times for a deeper hue and press before determining the final color.

🖎 Change the style, shorten or lengthen the dress, alter or remove the sleeves, remove the collar, or lower the neckline to give a new look to an older heirloom dress.

🖎 Use parts of a vintage or heirloom gown on a new gown. Use insets, lace trim, or even a detachable train from the older gown to complement the new dress.

Keeping the Gown in Perfect Condition

After purchasing the gown, having it made, or making it yourself, stuff the sleeves and bows with tissue paper to prevent hanging wrinkles. Cover the hanger with fabric scraps and hang the dress from the back of a door, curtain rod, or another high place. If the dress has a train with a ribbon loop, slip that over another hanger.

If the gown does not have them, stitch hanging tapes to the waistline and train so both will hang evenly:

1. Using seam binding or ½"-wide satin ribbon, cut two 32" lengths (or sections long enough to reach from the waistline to the shoulder when doubled) and one 10" length.

2. Baste together the cut edges of each ribbon piece.

3. Sew the ends of the two longer ribbons securely onto the waistline seam allowance at each sideseam with the ribbon loops hanging down (so they'll hang down when not being used).

4. Make thread loops, large enough for the ribbons to go through, just below each armhole seam. (Fig. 5-38)

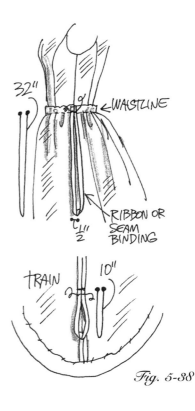

Fig. 5-38

5. Sew the remaining ribbon to the underside of the lower edge of the train's back seamline, high enough so it doesn't show when not in use.

A day or so before the wedding, place a clean sheet on the floor underneath the gown, unzip the bag, and spread out the train, letting any fold lines hang out. (Refer to page 117 for tips on heirlooming the gown after it is worn.)

CHAPTER SIX

Finishing Touches

Although the wedding dress is usually the focal point of the bride's ensemble, she must look terrific from head to toe. Her accessories should tie the entire look together, complement the dress design, and be in keeping with her own personal style.

Budget Helper

All of the accessories worn are important in perfecting the look, but they should not compete for attention. Often simple, less expensive accessories will look as good as or better than elaborate items.

In general, the bride should wear less lavish accessories with a highly ornate gown and more eye-catching ones with a simpler dress. They should be appropriate for the scale and shape of the dress, balancing the entire effect. For inspiration, look at the wide variety of unique accessory ideas featured in bridal magazines and at bridal shops.

Elegant Headpieces

You'll find as many options for headpieces, varying from simple elegance to elaborate creations, as there were when you were selecting the gown. Fabric, trims, ribbons, streamers, bows, and flowers are used to embellish them. And often a headpiece is the anchor for a veil that can be selected from a variety of styles and lengths. (Fig. 6-1)

You can purchase a headpiece, make one by decorating a pre-shaped form, or start from scratch by shaping and covering your own design. In any case, be sure that the headpiece fits perfectly and is comfortable to wear.

Budget Helper

Many headpieces purchased in full-retail bridal shops cost $100 and up—an average of $150 to $300! Because this is an item that will be worn only once, look for less expensive alternatives. Check at resale or consignment shops for comparable styles, consider renting one for a fraction of the retail cost, or make one yourself.

If you can glue or sew, it's not difficult to make an attractive

headpiece. Only minimal time and skill are required. If your time, interests, or confidence discourage this approach, hire a dressmaker—you'll still save a lot! A preshaped headpiece from a fabric or craft store is only about $5. Veiling is approximately $2 to $4 per yard. Flowers, beading, and lace are available for much, much less. You can make the perfect headpiece to coordinate with the dress and avoid the shopping hassle. It's even easy to make one that resembles a designer original.

A glue gun is ideal for covering and attaching most trims to a headpiece. It will eliminate any unnecessary wiring or sewing and the glue dries quickly. Read the handy tips on page 130 to help you use a glue gun most effectively.

FORMAL BEADED TIARA

SIMPLE BOW WREATH

Fig. 6-1

Selecting the style

When choosing the headpiece style, consider the formality of the wedding and the design of the wedding dress. Also decide what hairstyle the bride will wear on her wedding day because it will be important when selecting the headpiece. For a formal wedding, longer hair in an upswept style and a more elaborate headpiece would be appropriate. Long hair worn down with fresh flowers or a simple headband could be attractive for a less formal affair.

Sanity Saver

The hairstyle chosen should be one that will last through the ceremony and celebration that follows. When having the hair styled for the wedding, take the headpiece and veil along to make sure the hairstyle works well with them.

Types of headpieces available include a cap, wreath or ring, headband, crown or tiara, hat, bow, or floral spray. (Fig. 6-2) Many of these are held securely onto the head with a plastic comb or combs. Attach white or clear combs to any finished headpiece, even a purchased one, by hand-sewing, wiring with a lightweight covered floral wire, or tying with a 1/8"-wide white ribbon.

Fig. 6-2

You may want to go to a bridal shop and try on different styles to determine which looks best on you. Wear your hair as you will on your wedding day, as this will be a factor not only on how it looks but also how it fits.

Most headpieces are made to fit on the crown of the head, but the placement can vary if another position is more flattering. Consider these factors when selecting the headpiece style:

The hairstyle and face shape—A headpiece should frame the face and not hide it. A more detailed headpiece looks best with a simple hairstyle. A

wreath will complement an oval face, while a crown or tiara will give the illusion of height.

The personality of the bride—A regal, sophisticated bride may want to wear an elegantly simple headpiece, while a bride with a softer, romantic personality might choose one with lots of ruffles, flowers, or other detailing. (Fig. 6-3)

Fig. 6-3

The type of ceremony and reception—The headpiece and veil should be comfortable and easy to handle during the ceremony. If they'll be worn during the reception, ease of movement (especially if there will be dancing) should be considered.

Fresh flowers can be worn as a spray in the hair or used to decorate any headpiece style. Ribbon bows and streamers are often used along with the flowers. When using fresh flowers on the headpiece, also think about these options:

🍃 Select flowers to match the bridal bouquet.

🍃 Mix the flowers with herbs, used to symbolize good luck in the marriage.

🍃 Mix evergreens with flowers for a winter or Christmas wedding.

🍃 Add flowers and ribbon streamers to a ribbon wreath that is worn tied around the head.

Preshaped backings

Preshaped forms for caps, wreaths, and bands are available in craft and fabric stores to use as the base for a headpiece. These are made from a variety of materials, including:

🍃 **Buckram**—A stiff fabric that will need to be covered.

🍃 **Mesh or open-weave**— Stiffened shapes with holes large enough to weave through ¼"-wide ribbon. They can be worn covered or uncovered.

🍃 **Satin**—A stiffened shape that doesn't need to be covered. (Fig. 6-4)

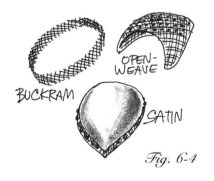

Fig. 6-4

BUCKRAM
OPEN-WEAVE
SATIN

Wire forms are also available, often in the traditional crown and wreath shapes, and need to be covered. Wrap and cover a crown form with stiff horsehair braid for stability before adding trim. Secure the braid by gluing. Allow it to dry and then trim the braid to match the shape. Add lace motifs and beading to conceal the wire.

Beaded wreath shapes are also available and come in different widths. They can be worn as purchased or decorated with additional floral or ribbon trim.

Hats made of stiff net, open-weave, or straw come in various shapes and are also popular. Satin hats are available, too. (Fig. 6-5) Most hats don't need to be covered but are usually embellished with laces, appliqués, ribbon, and flowers. For additional interest, weave narrow ribbon through open spaces to add color

NET DERBY

STRAW PICTURE HAT

SATIN PILLBOX

Fig. 6-5

and texture, wrap veiling or ribbon around the crown, or attach a veil.

Shaping your own

Shape a headband or wreath using 18-gauge wire, available at craft stores in 18" lengths or by the roll. The wire can be fabric-covered or plain. Form a headpiece using three strands of wire. Then wrap the shape with white floral tape and satin ribbon (if necessary), securing the ends with glue, and decorate as desired.

To make a headband, measure from ear to ear across the top of the head and cut the wire strands this length. After wrapping with floral tape and forming the shape, wrap it with ribbon and add decorations. Secure the band to the head by bending it to fit snugly or by hand-sewing a comb to it. (Fig. 6-6)

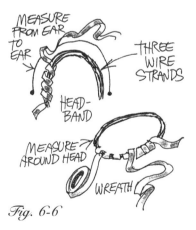

MEASURE FROM EAR TO EAR
THREE WIRE STRANDS
HEADBAND
MEASURE AROUND HEAD
WREATH

Fig. 6-6

For a wreath or other circular headpiece, measure around the head where it will be worn. If using precut lengths, twist two sections together comfortably around the head, then trim the ends, allowing 1½" for lapping.

Also allow ease for any trim wrapped around the headpiece. Make three circles this size and wrap them together with the tape and ribbon, beginning at a lapped area. Hand-sew a comb to secure the wreath to the head and decorate as desired. Shape the wreath to the head by bending the wires.

To vary a wreath or circular headpiece:

🍃 Use several strands of white chenille wire (available in craft stores), shaping them as above but twisting an additional chenille strand around the circle to strengthen it. Finish by wrapping with floral tape and ribbon before decorating.

🍃 When wrapping with the ribbon, leave long ribbon streamers at the back of the wreath.

🍃 Braid or knot ribbons before wrapping them.

🍃 Make a simple crown by overlapping silk floral spray stems 1½" to 2" and wrapping them with white floral tape. Then wrap and glue ¼"-wide satin ribbon over the stems. Attach a comb and an optional veil to the trimmed crown.

For the simplest headpiece, hand-sew a large bow and/or floral spray to a comb or barrette. See page 76 for simple bow instructions. Bows can be made from ribbon, fabric, or netting. For fabric bows, stiffen wide fabric strips with fabric stiffener or starch and tie them while damp. Cut a "V" in each end to prevent raveling.

> *❝If you're making the bride's and attendants' dresses or altering or shortening them, use the extra fabric to make flowers for the hair or to insert in the bouquet. They will be lasting remembrances of a special day. If you're beading the dress, use extra beads for the flower centers.❞*
>
> *Yvonne Perez-Collins*
> Soft Gardens (with detailed instructions for fabric flower making)

Covering a headpiece

If a headpiece needs to be covered, wrap and glue satin, taffeta, or ribbon over it. When gluing, test first to be sure the glue doesn't affect the fabric or ribbon. If necessary, hold the edges in place with a clothespin until the glue dries.

Remnants of wedding dress fabric, lace, or other coordinating fabric can be used to cover the shape. Cut the fabric cover on the bias for the best fit so that it can be shaped more easily over the curved surface. Stretch the fabric taut as you're gluing to shape it and smooth out the wrinkles. If necessary, clip and notch the edges to fit. (Fig. 6-7)

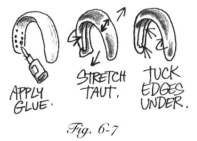

APPLY GLUE. STRETCH TAUT. TUCK EDGES UNDER.

Fig. 6-7

Trimming options

Most headpieces have some sort of embellishment. Many interesting trims are widely available, including all types of flowers, laces, beading, ribbons, and appliqués.

Consider these ornamentation ideas:

🍃 Glue small motifs from lace matching the wedding dress to a covered headpiece, adding beads after it is attached (see page 75). Any leftover appliqués are another good option.

🍃 Use attractive beading—strands, clusters, sprays, or individual beads are available.

🍃 Make flowers the focal point of a headpiece. Use larger flowers on the front and point others toward the center back. Fill the gaps with ribbons, beads, leaves, and/or baby's breath. The flowers may be real, silk, or rosettes made from fabric or ribbon. For information on rosettes and other trims, see pages 77, 127, and 129.

🍃 Make attractive fabric buds to trim any headpiece:

1. Cut a 2½" by 4" bias rectangle from satin, taffeta, or tulle for each bud. Fold in half lengthwise and curve the corners to form ovals. (Fig. 6-8)

2. Gather the cut edges tightly by sewing two rows of basting stitches close to the edges or serge, using a long stitch with the differential feed on a plus setting.

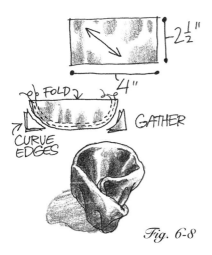

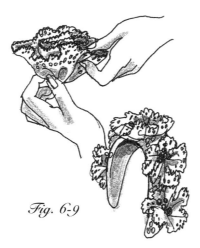

Fig. 6-9

Fig. 6-8

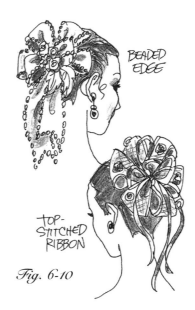

BEADED EDGE

TOP-STITCHED RIBBON

Fig. 6-10

3. Wrap and overlap the ends slightly to form the buds. Hand-sew or glue to secure the ends.

Construct pretty lace flowers from 4" to 6" lace doilies:

1. Apply heavy starch or fabric stiffener (available in craft stores) to the doilies by dipping or spraying.

2. Allow each doily to dry until damp, using a hair dryer to speed up the process.

3. Shape each doily into a flower, adjusting the edges to look like petals. (Fig. 6-9)

4. Allow the doilies to dry completely before attaching them to the headpiece.

Add purchased floral sprays or make your own by wrapping individual flower stems and leaves with white floral tape.

Decorate a bow's long edges by zigzagging over beading using a long, narrow zigzag stitch or a long serged rolled edge. Use a beading foot for easier application. Glue the beading ends securely and trim any excess when dry before tying into a bow. Or add color to the edges by serging over them with a rolled edge or by top-stitching on narrow satin ribbon to match the bridesmaids' dresses. (Fig. 6-10)

Make large, pouffy bows from veiling by forming loops and wrapping the center with white cloth-covered wire. Glue or hand-sew flowers or beading over the wire to cover it. (Fig. 6-11)

FORM LOOPS

COVERED WIRE

WRAP CENTER

Fig. 6-11

Frothy Veils

Most brides choose to wear some type of veil attached to an embellished headpiece—either a cap, hat, band, comb, tiara, wreath, or even a bow or spray of flowers. The veil not only complements the headpiece but also is an integral part of the bridal attire.

Choosing a fabric

Veiling fabrics are widely available and are sold by the yard. For the simplest veil, merely cut the fabric to the size and shape desired. The most popular veiling fabrics include:

Illusion—A very fine, delicate nylon netting, also called English net, that is very wide—up to 108". It is soft and strong and stretches in all directions, but it will not tear. Use it for full, gathered veils.

Tulle—Also a soft, fine nylon netting but stiffer and thicker than illusion. It ranges in width from 54" to 60" and is available in many colors, so it can be used for attendants' headpieces, too.

Lace—This yardage can be used for a mantilla veil, while lace trim can be used as a border for other veiling.

Deciding the style

Bridal veils are often double-layer, are worn from very short to very long, and can be made in several different styles (Fig. 6-12):

Fig. 6-12

Gathered or draped—The veiling is attached to a headpiece or comb.

Pouf—The veiling is more gathered and full, worn on the crown to add height. Shortened and shaped, it is also the most common style for a blusher veil, worn over the bride's face.

Mantilla—This style is not a headpiece but a circle of lace or veiling, from small to large, worn directly on the head.

Determining the size

Veil lengths and widths vary and should be scaled to the size of the bride and the wedding dress style. Lengths range from shoulder length to past the end of the train and are measured from the headpiece to the bottom edge. If you're uncertain about the best length, cut the veiling longer and shorten it after trying it on. Standard veil lengths are (Fig. 6-13):

Shoulder length—About 23" long, used when you want to emphasize the details on the dress back or in combination with a veil layer of another length. By itself, it is often worn with a less formal gown and needs 1½ yards of 72"-wide veiling.

Elbow or waist length—From 28" to 32" long, often used for a formal daytime wedding or with a shorter or informal dress. Use 1¾ yards of 72"-wide veiling.

Fingertip length—(Measured with arms straight.) From 45" to 50" long, worn with a long gown and the most popular length. Make one with 2¾ yards of 72"-wide veiling.

Floor or chapel length—From 80" to 90" long, used in semiformal and formal weddings. Use 5 yards of 108"-wide veiling.

Cathedral length—Approximately 108" long, used for a very formal wedding. It will

SHOULDER LENGTH

ELBOW LENGTH

FINGER-TIP LENGTH

CATHEDRAL LENGTH

FLOOR LENGTH

Fig. 6-13

extend 3 yards past the back waist and drapes onto the floor for at least 12" behind the train. This length will take 6 yards of 72"-wide veiling.

Determine how full you want the veil, depending on the width of the train and personal preference. Options include: 72" wide for a gathered or draped veil, 108" wide for a full veil, and 144" wide for a very full veil.

Making the veil

Pattern companies feature some veil patterns, but making one is simple. First decide the length you'll use. (Fig. 6-14) Then decide how many layers you'll have and determine the length of each—any layer added on top can be the same length but will look most attractive about 10" shorter than the one underneath it. Add the length of each layer to determine the total yardage.

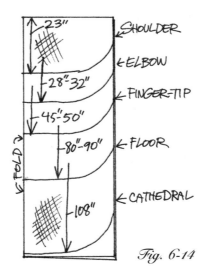

23"

28" 32"

45" 50"

80"-90"

108"

FOLD

SHOULDER
ELBOW
FINGER-TIP
FLOOR
CATHEDRAL

Fig. 6-14

Veiling has no grainline, so cutting is easy. Use sharp scissors or a rotary cutter and mat to

avoid jagged edges. Then fold and curve the edges as follows:

1. For a double-layer veil, fold the netting in half and then in half again. With the fold at the top, trim to curve the bottom corners. (Fig. 6-15)

FOLD TWICE

FOLD

FOLD

Fig. 6-15

2. Don't cut the separate tiers but simply refold them so the top layer is 10" above the underlayer.

3. For a gathered veil, sew gathering stitches ¼" away from the top edge. To form a pouf, sew gathering stitches approximately 6" to 10" from the fold (the measurement from the fold will be the width of the pouf). (Fig. 6-16) To gather, use one of the following methods:

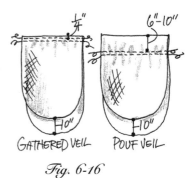

¼"

6"-10"

10"

10"

GATHERED VEIL

POUF VEIL

Fig. 6-16

Hand-gather using buttonhole twist.

Sew two rows of long basting stitches using a sewing machine and draw them up.

Zigzag or serge-flatlock with a long, wide stitch over, but not through, a filler thread such as crochet thread or buttonhole twist. Pull up the filler to gather.

Try different placements of the veil on the headpiece for the best look. The veil is usually placed with the gathered edge just under the back of the headpiece, but it can be anywhere on it. Hand-tack the gathers with long basting stitches or use a glue gun. A veil can also be made detachable and later removed for the reception—use *Velcro* with the soft side on the headpiece and the hooked side on the veil gathers. If the gathering stitches show, cover them with trim. If the veil is not being attached to a headpiece, fold and hand-sew the gathered edge to the underside and sew on combs to hold it in place.

Carefully press a veil using low heat and a dry iron, but test first on scraps of the veiling fabric.

Adding special trims

Good veiling does not need to be trimmed—even the most expensive veil can be simply cut to size. Trims may be used, however, to coordinate with the dress.

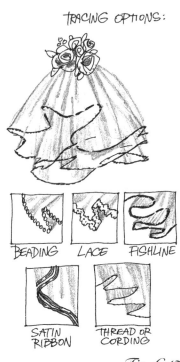

TRACING OPTIONS:

BEADING LACE FISHLINE

SATIN RIBBON THREAD OR CORDING

Fig. 6-17

Add the trimming before gathering. Consider these trim options (Fig. 6-17):

Sew lace trim around the veil edges. Top-stitch the lace right side up to the right side of the veiling, using a straight stitch or a long, narrow zigzag. On a circular veil, butt and zigzag the lace ends together.

Top-stitch or serge-seam one or more rows of ⅛"- or ¼"-wide satin ribbon to the edge of the veiling. The ⅛" width works better around sharper curves. To finish ribbon ends, turn ⅜" to the wrong side and hand-sew or zigzag, using a narrow stitch.

For a shiny edging, sew around the sides and bottom using rayon thread in the needle of a sewing machine or the upper looper of a serger. This is called tracing. Use woolly nylon for a denser, softer, nonshiny edge. When tracing with a sewing machine, zigzag over the edge using a narrow stitch, then stitch again with a slightly wider satin-length zigzag. When serging the edge, use a short, narrow balanced or rolled-edge stitch. For a softly ruffled edge, stretch as you zigzag or serge.

Trace the edge over cording for a more pronounced effect. Zigzag using a long, narrow stitch or serge with a rolled-edge or balanced stitch.

Trace over beading or narrow trim for an elegant look or over clear fishline for a ruffled edge, using the same stitch as above. For the ruffled edge, leave a 12" tail of fishline at both ends. Stretch after stitching to ripple the edge.

Scatter beads, lace motifs, or flowers on the veiling. Hand-sew them or glue them on using a strong, quick-drying embellishment glue that dries clear (test first). When gluing, place wax paper beneath the veiling and leave it in place until the glue dries.

Machine embroider a design on the veil, using scraps of water-soluble stabilizer on the back side while stitching.

Pretty Petticoats

A full petticoat is essential to shape and support a wedding gown's full skirt and should be the same silhouette. Also use a petticoat to lengthen a borrowed dress that is too short—the bottom ruffle can blend attractively with the skirt. Many bridal shops will rent a petticoat but check early, especially in the busiest wedding seasons, because they usually have only a few available.

Budget Helper

Save money by easily making a petticoat from any basic pattern. Or simply add ruffled rows of inexpensive stiff netting, such as crinoline, to a purchased half-slip.

It is important to try on the gown with the slip before hemming because the amount of fullness will affect the length of the dress. When making a petticoat, keep in mind that netting is scratchy when worn next to the skin, so sew the ruffles onto fabric.

Pouffy Pull-on Petticoat

Make a pretty, ruffled half-slip from inexpensive acetate, batiste, or other lightweight woven fabric and add four tiers of net ruffles. Use a basic pull-on A-line skirt pattern, lengthening it if necessary and widening the lower edge to at least 60". (Fig. 6-18)

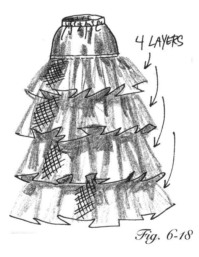

4 LAYERS

Fig. 6-18

MATERIALS NEEDED

Woven slip fabric, following the yardage requirements on the back of the pattern envelope and allowing for any extra length and width

Elastic, following the pattern requirements

2½ yards of 72"-wide stiff netting, such as crinoline

Optional: 14 yards of flat lace, ¼"-wide satin ribbon, horsehair braid, or clear fishline (see step 2)

CUTTING DIRECTIONS

Cut out the skirt, adjusting the pattern as described above.

Cut four ruffle strips 12" wide by the width of the netting.

HOW-TOS

Sew or serge all seams using ¼" allowances.

1. Make the slip, following the pattern instructions. Finish the lower edge 1" shorter than the dress, using a narrow hem, lace trim, or a narrow serged rolled edge or balanced stitch. Do not finish the elastic waistline application.

2. *Optional:* For an attractive, unsnaggable finish, top-stitch flat lace or ¼"-wide satin ribbon to one long edge of each net strip. Or serge-finish using a narrow, balanced or rolled-edge stitch to soften the edge. To add additional shaping, top-stitch horsehair braid to the lower edge of each tier. Another option for even more fullness is to zigzag or serge over fishline, stretching the edges after applying it.

3. Sew or serge each tier into a circle. Gather the upper edge, using one of the techniques on page 88. Pin the first ruffle to the slip so that it ends at the hemline, then

top-stitch it on over the gathering stitches. (Fig. 6-19) Repeat for the three additional tiers, lapping the lower edges of each one about 3" over the top edge of the previous ruffle, adjusting for the length of the slip.

Fig. 6-19

4. Try on the slip to check the length. Make any necessary adjustments before applying the elastic, following the pattern instruction.

Attractive Shoes and Hosiery

When selecting shoes for the bridal ensemble, consider the best height for comfort and for standing next to the groom. The bride should choose a height she's used to wearing, and she should try walking in the shoes before purchasing them. When shopping, take a sample of the gown fabric for color-matching, especially if it is off-white or ivory.

Budget Helper

Shoes, especially those with fabric uppers, can be easily embellished for a one-of-a-kind bridal accessory. Simply use a glue gun to apply lace motifs matching the dress, beading, or small floral pieces. (Fig. 6-20)

Break in the shoes before the wedding and bring another comfortable pair to the reception, especially if there will be lots of dancing.

Fig. 6-20

“*Consider lower to mid-height, rather than high heeled shoes, for the bride and attendants. Tottering down a long aisle, in heel heights seldom worn otherwise, can cause embarrassment and additional nervousness, all often captured on videotape for posterity.*”

Gail Brown
Gail Brown's All-New Instant Interiors

Choose hosiery that complements both the dress and the shoes, especially when wearing a dress shorter than floor length. Also remember that the hosiery will show if the garter is removed during the reception. Sheer off-white hose usually blend better with a white dress than stark white. Be sure to have one or two spare pair available for the ceremony and reception.

“*Make a tiny case from extra wedding-dress fabric to hold a brand-new penny (minted the same year as the wedding) for the bride's father to give her as the 'lucky penny' worn in her shoe.*”

Yvonne Perez-Collins
Soft Gardens

Other Accessory Options

Depending on tradition and personal preference, several other accessories will usually be included in the bride's attire. A garter, small bag, prayer book or Bible, flowers (see page 24), jewelry, and even a pretty handkerchief are small details that can add a finishing touch.

> **"***I wish I had had the foresight to make a pretty white quilted or crocheted shawl to throw over my shoulders on my wedding day. Although we were married in August, I should have known to anticipate a damp day with a high temperature in the 40s on the upper peninsula of Michigan the day we were wed!***"**
>
> *Kathleen Eaton*
> Stitch 'n' Quilt

Garters

A garter is usually worn as part of the bride's outfit. Inexpensive (but very attractive) ones are available in bridal shops and mail-order catalogs—you may want to purchase an extra to throw after the ceremony. Embellishments, such as small rosettes and ribbon, can be added for a personal touch (see page 126). Adding a blue ribbon bow may be the "something blue" of the traditional requirements.

Bridal bags

Easily make and/or embellish a pretty little bridal bag to carry makeup for touch-ups, money, and a handkerchief. If purchasing a bag, look for a plain satin one, such as a drawstring style, that is easily carried and matches or blends with the gown color. Add lace motifs to match the dress, pearls, beading, or other coordinating trims. (Fig. 6-21)

Fig. 6-21

Gloves

Although gloves used to be considered a bridal necessity, they are now an option. If gloves will be worn, select a simple design if the dress is elaborate. The fabric and color should be as similar to the dress as possible. Buy the gloves a half size too large so they will slip off easily before exchanging rings.

Determine the glove length by the dress sleeve length: wear wrist-length gloves with long sleeves, below-the-elbow length with short sleeves, and over-the-elbow length with sleeveless styles. (Fig. 6-22)

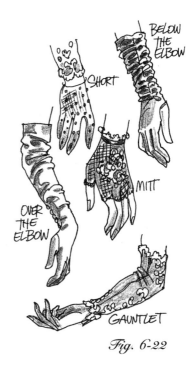

Fig. 6-22

Mitts or gauntlets of lace, georgette, or other trimmed fabric are also an option—they leave the fingers uncovered for the ring exchange. Embellish any plain gloves or mitts by sewing on ribbon roses, pearls, lace, and bows to coordinate with the wedding outfit.

Jewelry

The jewelry worn by the bride is usually a very personal decision. It is often small and delicate to complement, but not fight with, the look of the gown.

Traditionally the bride wears family heirlooms and/or a gift from the groom. Pearls, lockets, cameos, and other sentimental treasures are all favorites. Any jewelry should be in scale and keeping with the entire ensemble, and simplicity is best—if in doubt, leave it off.

Handkerchiefs

A delicate trimmed handkerchief is another optional wedding accessory and a wonderful keepsake of the special day. Add the bride's monogram by hand- or machine-embroidery to personalize it even more.

> "Tacking a few simple folds can change the bride's hankie into a charming bonnet for her first baby."
>
> *Gaye Kriegel* co-author
> Affordable Heirlooms

Beautiful Bridal Handkerchief

Make a pretty but practical bridal accessory. Use antique linens and laces or fabrics from the wedding gown for a very special remembrance. (Fig. 6-23)

Fig. 6-23

MATERIALS NEEDED

One 8" square of soft lightweight linen, batiste, or Swiss cotton

One yard of antique lace or 1½"-wide flat Venice lace trim with one scalloped edge (the lace must be flexible enough to be applied easily on a curved edge)

Small pearl beads

Washable fabric or embellishment glue

CUTTING DIRECTIONS

Fold the fabric square in half and in half again and round the corners.

HOW-TOS

1. Finish all edges by folding ⅛" to the wrong side twice and hand-sewing or finish them with a narrow serged rolled edge.

2. Place the lace edge over the hanky hem, lapping the lace ends ¼" at one corner after turning the top end under ¼" and the lower end up ¼" with the raw edges sandwiched in between. Top-stitch the lace to the hanky close to the edge using a straight or narrow zigzag stitch.

3. Secure the lapped lace edges by zigzagging over the folds. (Fig. 6-24)

LAP & ZIGZAG.

Fig. 6-24

4. Add monogramming, if desired, by hand- or machine-embroidering on the corner opposite the lapped lace edges. Use water-soluble stabilizer on the underside when machine-embroidering and remove the excess afterward.

5. Glue a cluster of pearls at each hanky corner.

CHAPTER SEVEN

The Wedding Party

Selecting attendants for the wedding is one of the first big planning decisions. The choices can be very simple and uncomplicated or may require a great deal of tact and special consideration. The bride's sister or best friend is usually the maid or matron (if married) of honor, while the groom may select his brother or best friend as best man. In the south, tradition sometimes calls for the groom to select his father for the honor.

Attendants should be chosen out of love and respect, not because of a feeling of obligation. If the selection is difficult, both the bride and groom may have two maids or matrons of honor and best men. For an informal wedding in a home, chapel, or judge's chamber, it is appropriate to have only a maid or matron of honor and a best man to serve as witnesses and the best man may be the groom's father.

Other wedding attendants may include one or more bridesmaids, groomsmen, and ushers, chosen from among close friends. The number will depend on the size and formality of the wedding. Inviting the groom's sister to serve as a bridesmaid or the bride's brother as a groomsman or usher can be a thoughtful gesture toward future family relations.

"Wanting my three-year-old son from a previous marriage to feel especially involved in my wedding, I asked him if there was something special that he wanted to wear. He decided on a black Bat Man cape for the reception, worn over his pants and jacket! He loved it and felt very important with all of the attention he received."

Jan Saunders
Jan Saunders' Wardrobe Quick-Fixes

Fig. 7-1

For a more formal wedding, you may also include children: a ring bearer is usually between the ages of three and six and a flower girl is between the ages of four and ten. (Fig. 7-1) Any child older than eight can be a candle lighter, junior bridesmaid, or junior groomsman.

Sanity Saver

Decide early whether you want to include children in the wedding. Especially young or precocious children can be real scene stealers. But they can also add to the wedding happiness and festivities, especially if they are children from a previous marriage or very close to the bride and groom.

Occasionally someone must decline the honor of being selected as a member of the wedding party due to other obligations or for lack of time or funds. Each situation must be handled with understanding and grace. Compromises can be made so that the person can participate or another friend can be asked to fill in when someone declines or must drop out.

Who Does What?

Responsibilities accompany the honor of being an attendant. Each one is expected to pay for his or her attire, whether it is purchased, rented, or made to specifications.

Other responsibilities might be as easy as lighting candles or looking cute (for younger participants) or taking an integral part in the smooth running of the wedding. Traditionally, members of the wedding party often do the following:

Maid or matron of honor

The maid or matron of honor gives any needed support to the bride in the weeks before the wedding and on the wedding day. She is also invited to all the prenuptial parties. Her obligations may include:

🌸 Helping address invitations and shop for the wedding attire.

🌸 Arranging for the bridesmaids' fittings.

🌸 Organizing a girls' night out or other prenuptial party.

🌸 Assisting the bride on the wedding day by helping her dress and supervising the bridesmaids.

🌸 Holding the groom's ring during the ceremony until the ring exchange.

🌸 Adjusting the bride's veil and train and holding the bridal bouquet (and perhaps the gloves) during the ceremony. (Fig. 7-2)

Fig. 7-2

🌸 Signing the marriage license as an official witness.

🌸 Standing next to the groom in the receiving line at the reception.

🌸 Helping the bride change after the reception and notifying the parents when the couple is ready to leave so that they can come wish them well.

Best man

Next to the bride and groom, the best man is the most important person in the wedding party because he makes sure the wedding runs smoothly. His responsibilities may include:

🌸 Helping arrange for honeymoon travel or for any special going-away plans.

🌸 Hosting a bachelor dinner or organizing a bachelor party.

🌸 Helping the groom stay organized on the wedding day. Does he have the marriage license? Are all of his clothes and accessories in order for both the ceremony and for going away? (One groom we know, in his state of nervousness, accidentally brought the wrong pants for the ceremony. His best man had to fight his way frantically through twenty miles of busy city traffic to retrieve the matching ones before the ceremony could begin!)

🌸 Supervising the ushers and groomsmen.

🌸 Taking care of the bride's ring until the ring exchange.

🌸 Signing the marriage license as an official witness.

🌸 Handing the payments or honorariums to the clergyman and anyone else involved in the ceremony, such as an organist or other musician. The groom should put the money in envelopes in advance so the best man can unobtrusively hand them out after the ceremony.

🌸 Offering the first toast to the bride and groom at the reception.

☙ Returning the groom's outfit, if it was rented, after the wedding.

Bridesmaids

The bridesmaids will assist the bride when needed during the weeks before the ceremony and may join together to organize a shower for her. They'll also have their gowns fitted or made on schedule and join in the prenuptial celebrations. During the ceremony, they have no responsibilities other than to add to the festive occasion with their colorful dresses, bouquets, and warm good spirits.

Groomsmen and ushers

Although the terms "grooms-man" and "usher" are often used interchangeably, there is a distinction between the two. Groomsmen stand up with the groom during the ceremony and ushers seat the guests. Groomsmen often act as ushers and ushers may fill in as escorts to the bridesmaids if there is an uneven number of bridesmaids and groomsmen.

These men will greet the guests and seat them before the ceremony. They also will assist the bride's mother with any details before the ceremony and are responsible for transportation for the bridesmaids. Immediately before the ceremony, they will seat the mother of the groom and then the mother of the bride.

Extra ushers may be needed (in addition to the groomsmen) at a large wedding. The standard rule of thumb is one usher for every fifty guests. Ushers line up at the left of the entrance to the church and offer their right arm to escort a woman to her seat—usually on the left for the bride's family and friends and on the right for the groom's. Her husband, children, or others accompanying her will follow. Single men walk side by side with an usher to be seated.

Coordinating the Bridesmaids' Ensembles

The bride chooses her attendants' outfits, keeping in mind their budgets, personal style preferences, and figure types. She decides whether they will buy, rent, or have them sewn.

Sanity Saver

When shopping for a dress, don't take all the bridesmaids along at the same time—it will be almost impossible to get a consensus of opinion.

If the bride knows of a dressmaker, she may make arrangements for the dresses to be sewn, as well as scheduling the first fitting appointments.

Design

After selecting her own dress design, the bride should select complementary bridesmaid dresses. Bridal patterns often have coordinating designs for the attendants, ensuring the same degree of formality. (Fig. 7-3)

The attendants' hems should be the same distance from the floor and the same length or shorter than the bride's—never longer. A cocktail or tea length, several inches above the ankle, is the most versatile. If possible, look for a design that can be worn again or at least redone so that it can be worn again. Easy alterations may be to shorten the dress or remove embellishments.

Fig. 7-3

Many of the dresses now are of simpler design, with less trim and beading.

Two-piece outfits, sheaths, and separates are the easiest to fit and the most flattering for the majority of figure types and ages. For the fuller figure, longer, fuller skirts, V-necklines, and dropped waistlines are the most flattering.

Variations may be made in the bridesmaid dresses for different figure types or for distinguishing between them and the maid or matron of honor. For originality, you might:

🌢 Consider different styles in the same color and fabric.

🌢 Use two-piece outfits and vary only the tops, especially if the attendants have different figure types. (Fig. 7-4)

🌢 Select identical dresses with variations in color or with contrasting trim. The maid or matron of honor's dress may have added embellishment, such as ruffles.

🌢 For an older bridesmaid, select a dress she will feel comfortable wearing—perhaps the same color and dress length but not necessarily the same design.

Color

The bridesmaids' dresses make the strongest color impact of the wedding. They may be all the same, different shades of the same color, or different colors for each dress. Traditionally deeper colors are worn for winter and pastel colors are worn for summer, but today anything goes. During the

Fig. 7-4

Christmas season and at prom time, you'll find even more dresses that are appropriate for weddings.

Other considerations include:

🌢 The dress colors should coordinate with flowers of the season.

🌢 The color chosen should be easy to match or coordinate with shoes, ribbons, and decorations.

🌢 The color should look good in the church or other ceremony location, especially for photography.

🌢 The color should be becoming to the attendants.

🌢 The maid or matron of honor may be distinguished by a differ-

ent dress color or with a different color floral bouquet.

Selecting the dresses

Bridal shops have a limited selection of dresses, so shop and order early—at least two to four months in advance. Allow at least two weeks for alterations. Be sure each bridesmaid receives a written receipt.

Budget Helper

If you're ordering all the dresses in the same color and design, ask for a discount from the store.

Other options include renting the dresses, purchasing them from a discount or outlet store, or having them made (see page 66). If there is only one attendant, she may wear a dress she already owns or borrow one that is appropriate in color and design.

Sewing the dresses

When the dresses are sewn to your specifications, they will be in the design and fabric you've chosen and less expensive than if they were special-ordered. If possible, and if the bridesmaids' budgets allows, have one dressmaker sew all the gowns so that they all will look the same and the lengths will be coordinated. If a change is made in the design, one dressmaker can do it much more efficiently than having to give extensive instructions to individual dressmakers (and hope that they'll understand). The fit of each professionally sewn dress can be perfect because a fitting muslin can be made for the bodice or the entire dress.

Headpieces

The bridesmaids may wear any type of headpiece (see page 82 for ideas), but it should not be more elaborate than the one worn by the bride. Sometimes a headpiece is eliminated all together, leaving more emphasis on the hair style.

(see page 82 for ideas)

> ### Budget Helper
>
> If you make the headpieces, refer to the suggestions in Chapter 6. The costs can be minimal, even for ones that look like designer originals.

Think about one of these fashionable options:

🎀 Make bows made from the bridesmaid dress fabric.

🎀 Add a short veil to headbands or other headpieces.

🎀 Use hats with flowers and ribbons matched to the dresses.

🎀 Choose a spray of flowers, ribbons, or a combination of the two. (Fig. 7-5)

🎀 Create identical headpieces in different colors, especially if the dresses are different colors.

Other accessories

Watches or bracelets are usually not worn by the bridesmaids to prevent detracting from the pol-

Fig. 7-5

ished look or from catching them on any flowers they are carrying. All bridesmaids should wear the same or very similar earrings and/or necklaces.

Dyed-to-match shoes are no longer a necessary part of the attendants' attire, but if they are used, they should all be dyed at the same time to ensure a perfect color match. You may choose to have the attendants wear their own plain pumps or other coordinating shoes. However, they should all be the same color, height, and style.

Coordinate the hosiery with the dress color, with all attendants wearing the same color. Be sure that extra pairs are available at the wedding and reception, in case of runs or snags.

If the bride wants to ensure a matching, coordinated look and can afford it, she may choose to give some or all of the accessories to her attendants. Earrings or necklaces are common gifts. Headpieces, shoes, hosiery, gloves, and even matching lipstick and nail polish are sometimes purchased by the bride.

The Groom and Male Attendants

The style of men's clothing is determined by the formality of the bride's dress and of the wedding, the time of day, and the season of the year. It can be as traditional or as casual as you wish. (Fig. 7-6)

Fig. 7-6

All of the men dress alike, including the fathers of the bride

and groom. The groom (and perhaps the best man) is distinguished by the color of his tie, type of accessory (vest instead of cummerbund), or the color or flower of his boutonnière. The groom can wear the same color as his attendants or a contrasting color jacket and/or pants.

Dark suits may be worn for a less formal wedding, saving the cost of renting formalwear. Especially if the colors are coordinated, they will look very much alike. If a groomsman or usher does not have a suit that is appropriate, he can probably borrow one from a friend.

Traditional men's wedding attire is usually rented from a tuxedo shop. Shoes can be rented for an additional fee, but to save money and provide more comfort, you may choose to have the men wear their own if they are all similar in style and coordinate with the attire. Register the wedding and the style of attire chosen at the tuxedo shop under

the name of the bride and groom, as well as the date of the wedding. The men can come in at any time to be measured.

Budget Helper

Some shops will not charge for the groom's rental if several other outfits are rented from them. Be sure to inquire.

Menswear fashions change and any reputable tuxedo shop can help you choose the style that will be best for the occasion. In general, however, tradition calls for some style of formalwear if the wedding is formal or even semiformal.

Cummerbunds and ties can be color-matched to the bridesmaid dresses and are often made from brocade or tapestry. Patterns are available for these accessories if the shop doesn't have the exact fabric or color you want. Coordinating boutonnieres are pinned on the left lapel.

The Mothers' Attire

The bride's mother sets the style of the mothers' outfits by selecting hers first. She should then inform the groom's mother so that she can choose something similar.

The mothers' apparel should be in keeping with the formality of the wedding and be less formal than the bridal party. The styles need not be coordinated with the attendants and can be street or floor length, dress or suit, but no longer than those in the bridal party. The colors should blend with the color scheme of the wed-

Fig. 7-7

ding and not detract from the wedding gown. Also keep in mind how the dresses or suits will look in photographs.

Bridal shops have a limited selection of dresses for mothers, but a better choice is found in department stores or dress shops. Each mother should select something to suit both her personality and her needs beyond the wedding. Suits are popular because they are comfortable and flattering for most figure types. (Fig. 7-7) Choose the fabric for ease in wearing as well as appearance.

Junior Attendants

One or more junior attendants may be included in the wedding and their parents are usually expected to pay for their attire. They should wear outfits coordinating with the wedding party but in a design suitable for their age. A junior bridesmaid or flower girl may wear the same color as the bridesmaids, a lighter tone of the same color, or the color of the bride's dress.

Flower girl

The flower girl walks ahead of the bride in the wedding processional and traditionally tosses rose petals from a decorated basket as she walks down the aisle. This tradition has been changed to carrying a basket of flowers because

Budget Helper

It's not always necessary to buy or rent a special outfit for a flower girl or junior bridesmaid. Often a party dress, even one she already owns, can be embellished with the wedding colors and will look great. (Fig. 7-8)

of the possibility of slipping on the petals.

Baskets of different shapes can be used, but the one chosen shouldn't be too large. It should have a tall handle that is easy to carry and should be decorated in white and/or the wedding colors, often with ribbon streamers.

Fig. 7-8

Although florists will decorate a basket and arrange the flowers, you can easily do it yourself, using fabrics, trims, and flowers to match the wedding party. (See page 52 for other basket ideas.)

Festive Flower Basket

Choose one of several simple options for decorating a pretty basket for the flower girl to carry. (Fig. 7-9)

Fig. 7-9

MATERIALS NEEDED

One small round basket with sides and a tall handle

One piece of lace, organdy, tulle, or satin at least 3" larger than the inside of the basket

1/4"-wide or wider ribbon, either in a wedding color or white

A glue gun (see page 130 for tips)

Optional: Paper-backed fusible transfer web

Optional: Tulle, wired beading, pearl beading, wired ribbon, and/or ruffled lace

Optional: One lace or crocheted doily approximately 3" larger than the inside of the basket

CUTTING DIRECTIONS

Measure the inside of the basket and add 3". (Fig. 7-10)

Cut a circle of this measurement from the fabric. If cutting it from lace, follow the lace motifs to avoid any finishing.

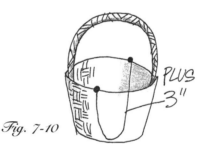

Fig. 7-10

HOW-TOS

1. Finish the outer edges of the fabric circle, using one of the following methods:

   a. Fuse a 1/4"-wide strip of transfer web to the outside of the circle, folding the edge over to make a quick hem.

   b. Serge-finish the circle with a narrow rolled edge.

   c. Attach beading by zigzagging or serging over it using a long, narrow stitch.

   d. Top-stitch narrow lace to the circle's outside edge.

   e. A lace or tulle circle does not need to be finished.

2. Place the liner loosely in the basket. (Or use the optional doily as a liner.) It will be held in place by the floral arrangement.

3. Wrap the ribbon around the basket handle and glue the ends to secure them. Further embellish the basket, using one or more of the following ideas:

   a. Tie ribbon bows or strips of tulle around the base of the handles.

   b. Glue wired ribbon to the basket rim. (Fig. 7-11)

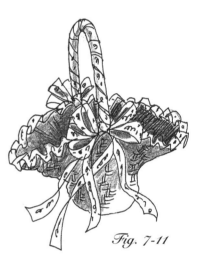

Fig. 7-11

   c. Add ribbon streamers, knotting the ends.

Ring bearer

The ring bearer often dresses the same as the groomsmen, but he may wear short pants. If he has a good dress-up suit, you may decide to have him wear that. It should be dark for a winter ceremony or lighter for summer. A very young ring bearer might be cute wearing white shorts and shirt with a bow tie. He traditionally will precede the flower girl down the aisle and leave side by side with her right behind the bride and groom.

The ring bearer's responsibility is to carry the rings on a pillow for the ring exchange. Because of the importance of the rings in the ceremony and considering his age, it's best to tie fake rings to the pillow. The best man and matron of honor will take responsibility for the actual rings.

The ring bearer's pillow can be any shape—round, square, or heart-shaped, and should be approximately 10" to 12" in size. One easy option is to purchase a small satin baby or doll pillow and embellish it yourself. Hand-sew or glue ruffled lace around the outside of the pillow, adding ribbon bows and streamers at the corners. Attach floral sprays, lace motifs, or appliqués on top of the pillow for decoration. To tie on each ring, fold a 12" length of ⅛"-wide ribbon in half. Hand-sew or glue the center point to the pillow.

So the pillow can be carried easily, hand-sew 3" of ½"-wide elastic lace to the underside, tucking each end under. (Fig. 7-12)

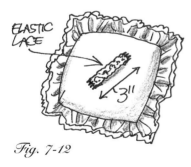

Fig. 7-12

It is also simple to quickly cover a small pillow before embellishing it:

For a small round pillow, cut a circle of fabric 2½ times larger than a pillow form. Finish the edge of the circle using one of the techniques described for the

Flower Basket on page 100. Pull up the fabric tightly around the pillow and secure the edges with a rubber band. (Fig. 7-13) Arrange the fullness evenly. Tie a ribbon around the gathers, knotting the rings near the center and leaving streamers. Attach an elastic holder to the underside.

Fig. 7-13

For a small square pillow, wrap fabric or a hand towel around a small form. Knot the opposite corners and tuck the ends under. Cover the knot with lace motifs, an appliqué, a floral spray, or ribbon bows. Attach ribbons to tie on the rings and sew an elastic holder to the underside. (Fig. 7-14)

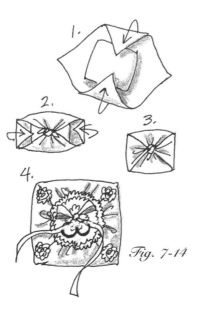

Fig. 7-14

Romantic Crocheted Ring Pillow

Quickly make a pretty ring bearer's pillow from two crocheted lace doilies. It will look like a treasured heirloom! (Fig. 7-15)

Fig. 7-15

MATERIALS NEEDED

Two 8" or 10" crocheted doilies (available in linen and craft stores)

Two taffeta or satin circles, 1" smaller than the doilies

Polyester fiberfill stuffing

1½ yards of ⅛"- or ¼"-wide ribbon in white or a wedding color

A tapestry needle

3½" of ½"-wide elastic lace

Ribbons, lace motifs, beading, and/or floral sprays

How-Tos

1. Place the fabric circles wrong sides together and seam ⅛" from the outer edges, leaving an opening for stuffing.

2. Fill the pillow with fiberfill and finish sewing it closed.

3. Sandwich the fabric pillow between the wrong sides of the two doilies. Sew the doily edges together, using the narrow ribbon threaded through the tapestry needle, and tie the ribbon ends into a bow.

4. Attach embellishments as desired and sew the elastic lace to the underside for a holder (see Fig. 7-12).

Junior bridesmaid or groomsman

When you want to include any children over eight years old in the wedding, invite them to be junior attendants as a special honor. Depending on their age, they may be treated exactly as any other attendant or their dress may be modified to suit their age in a color and style complementary to the rest of the wedding party.

A young junior bridesmaid usually comes down the aisle after the maid or matron of honor and before the ring bearer and flower girl. She leaves in the same order. She may or may not be escorted.

CHAPTER EIGHT

Setting the Scene

No matter where the ceremony and reception are being held, you'll need to give special thought to the atmosphere you want to create. Flowers, candles, and other romantic touches can all help set the perfect mood.

A church ceremony is often solemn and quietly elegant, while the reception may be fun-filled, lighthearted, and happy. Both should reflect your personality and the style of wedding that you've chosen. Flowers will usually play an important part; then a few easy-to-do final touches will help make the occasion truly memorable for years to come.

Decorating for the Ceremony and Reception

At both the ceremony site and the reception, you'll want to create a festive scene. Often the floral arrangements used for the ceremony are later taken to the reception so that they can be fully enjoyed throughout the day. Many of our ideas in this chapter can be used at one location or both.

All of your decorating needs a focal point, such as an attractive altar arrangement for the ceremony or the cake table at the reception. All of the other decorating will accentuate that focal point. Decorating for an elegant occasion may include only simple arrangements to enhance the natural beauty of a setting or you may want masses of plants and flowers, votive candles entwined with ivy, or lots of tiny white-light candles among yards of tulle.

Floral decorations

Fresh flowers add fragrance and freshness to the wedding day.

They should be in keeping with the wedding style and any theme you've chosen for the reception. (Fig. 8-1) Flowers can also drive the price of the wedding up faster than any other item.

Fig. 8-1

Budget Helper

Refer back to page 21 in Chapter 2 for advice on choosing suppliers and for other money-saving suggestions.

Coordinate all the flowers to complement the season, wedding colors, and sites for the ceremony and reception. Remember, though, that they are only accessories and should not upstage the entire affair.

The flowers traditionally used for a church ceremony might include an altar arrangement, baskets of flowers strategically placed, and other sturdy flowers for pew markers. A floral arch might be the focus of an outdoor wedding, while blossoms floating in the water could enhance a ceremony at poolside.

You may want to have additional flowers for the reception

because the time spent there will be longer than at the ceremony. If you'll be using some of the same arrangements for both, plan the reception decor so that the setting won't look completely barren before the shared flowers arrive.

A florist or floral designer can be hired to do all or part of the floral arrangements, making the flowers a major part of your entire budget. With that in mind, consider these ways to save on floral expenses and still have a beautiful wedding:

🌿 Choose a wedding date that is close to a holiday to make use of decorations already in place at the setting, such as poinsettias and trimmed trees during the Christmas holidays.

🌿 Consider sharing flowers with another couple having a wedding in the same place on the same day.

🌿 Rent, rather than buy, potted plants for decorating.

🌿 Ask a member of a garden club or students in a flower-arranging class to handle the floral decorations.

🌿 Solicit flowers from friends and neighbors.

🌿 Avoid exotic flowers and use only those in season.

🌿 Use more greenery, candles, and ribbon and fewer flowers in the arrangements. (Fig. 8-2)

Fig. 8-2

🌿 Mix fresh flowers with dried or silk ones.

🌿 Use all silk flowers instead of fresh, but remember it will cost the same to arrange them.

To keep flowers fresh, have them delivered to the ceremony and reception sites no more than two hours before the wedding. Make sure they're not exposed to severe heat or cold and handle them as little as possible because they can be damaged easily. Loose flowers and bouquets should be kept in water until they're used.

If you're in doubt about the type of floral arrangement you're ordering, ask to see a sample arrangement the week before the wedding. And don't hesitate to ask for volunteer help. Delegate someone to be responsible for the flowers and to make sure that they are all received and properly arranged. Or designate someone to pick them up if they're not being delivered.

Easy garlands

For additional decoration at either the ceremony or reception site, quickly make garlands or swags to decorate mantles, staircases, altars, or pews:

1. Wire together 5"- to 6"-long sections of greenery by overlapping them and wrapping the joined areas with florist wire to make any length you want.

2. Mist the greenery and place it in a plastic bag punched with holes until it is needed.

3. Add fresh flower accents immediately before the ceremony or reception. (Fig. 8-3)

Fig. 8-3

As an option to greenery, make garlands from inexpensive netting or tulle yardage, attaching bows at regular intervals. Or add small arrangements of flowers and baby's breath to the garland, tied with tulle or ribbon.

The bridal bouquet

Before ordering the bridal bouquet, check bridal magazines for ideas and current trends and for suggestions on mixing colors as well as flowers. Take a picture of your favorite types of flowers when ordering from a florist or floral designer. Traditionally the bouquet is white or mainly white and sweet smelling.

The wedding gown should be the focus at the ceremony—not the flowers. So consider the style and texture of the gown when making your floral selection. If the gown is intricate, a single flower tied with a ribbon might be the most appropriate. With a gown that has a simple design in the front, a more elaborate bouquet may be a better choice. The flowers can be tied or wired together or placed in a plastic bouquet holder. (Fig. 8-4)

Fig. 8-4

Budget Helper

Instead of carrying a bouquet, the bride may choose to carry a family Bible with a fresh flower and ribbon streamers or a rosary, a fan with a small floral arrangement attached, a simple spray, or simply nothing at all. (Fig. 8-5)

Fig. 8-5

The bridal bouquet is traditionally placed on the cake table as a decoration during the reception.

Attendants' flowers

The bridesmaid bouquets should be coordinated with the bride's in style, proportion, and color, but these bouquets are smaller in size. The color of the flowers and ribbon should coordinate with the dress they're wearing, and should blend with it, rather than totally match, so that it will stand out. The maid or matron of honor sometimes carries a bouquet that is different in color, but the same style, as the other attendants.

To transport bouquets easily to the reception, place the stems into *Styrofoam* to prevent crushing the flowers or bows.

Instead of bouquets, bridesmaids may carry floral arrangements in baskets (Fig. 8-6), muffs decorated with flowers for a winter wedding, or leis around their necks in the tropics. Another option is to have them wear floral wreaths or crowns as a headpiece, but the flowers used must be sturdy enough to remain intact through the ceremony and reception.

Fig. 8-6

The men in the wedding party wear boutonnieres with the groom's being different from those of the other men. Boutonnieres should be a single blossom or bud matching one of the bridal bouquet flowers and about 4" long.

Flower-arranging tips

You may decide to arrange some or all of the wedding flowers yourself and feature your own original designs. Consider the size, texture, and shape of the flowers you choose, using a larger flower as the focal point for each arrangement or bouquet and filling in with small and medium-size flowers.

"Harden" or "condition" the flowers so that they will last longer. They should be soaked so the stems, blossoms, and leaves are all filled with water:

1. Strip the stems of any leaves that will be in water.

2. Cut the stem ends on an angle at the desired length

3. Submerge the stem ends into deep buckets of 70° to 75° water that has a preservative added.

4. Leave the flowers in water at room temperature for approximately two hours. Soak greenery for at least one day.

5. Keep both in a cool place after soaking.

Silk flowers are a popular choice for floral arrangements because they will not wilt, do not cause hay fever, and are difficult to damage. They can be freshened by shaking them in a bag with salt. Silk flowers are also often used in a special bouquet made for tossing at the reception.

Floral tape and foam, available from any floral or craft-supply store, are essential for flower

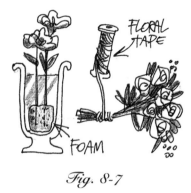

Fig. 8-7

arranging. (Fig. 8-7) Floral tape comes in green and white and, when stretched, becomes tacky and sticks to itself. It's used to wrap around flowers, greens, and wire to cover them and hold them in place. The ends are sealed by simply pressing them to the stems.

Special foam, used for arranging silk and dry flowers, is firm and doesn't crumble. Cut it with a serrated knife or fine wire to a size that will fit the arrangement container. When using a foam for fresh flowers, soak it in water until it sinks, then place it in the container and tape or hot glue it in place before arranging.

Make small floral arrangements by winding floral tape around flowers or bunches of flowers and the traditional baby's breath, adding ribbon bows and streamers. Dried flowers, such as those from a bridal shower, can be made into floral arrangements well ahead of time. Fresh roses and baby's breath are often used to fill in dried arrangements.

Flowers with long, tall stalks work well for free-form arrangements, made just before the wedding. Reinforce or lengthen any stem by placing 20-gauge wire

next to it and wrapping with floral tape to the end of the wire. This works well if the stem is too flimsy and cannot be controlled in the arrangement or needs to be held in place.

When using flowers on top of the wedding cake, engage the florist for the job, not the caterer. A florist knows the types of flowers appropriate for an edible cake and how to arrange them. Fresh flowers can also be tied onto the cake knife and toasting glasses with white satin ribbon and used in the table centerpieces.

Aisle runner

Some churches or wedding consultants may suggest that you use a white aisle runner for the wedding ceremony. If so, the guests will be seated from the sides rather than the center of the church.

Budget Helper

Today the custom of having an aisle runner is not necessary, even for the most formal wedding, so save the extra expense. The stark white runner may not complement the bride's dress and will not be the best background if photos are being taken.

Pew decorations

For a church ceremony, decorations usually include some type of pew bows or arrangements. They can be on all pews or on alternating pews and are either white or coordinated with the wedding colors. Greens or floral sprays may also be attached to the pews, or wider aisles can be lined with pots of flowers or greenery embellished with ribbon bows.

Large bows, visible from three sides, are the most traditional pew decorations. (Fig. 8-8) They may be purchased from a florist ready-made but are simple to make so that you can personalize them with your own individual design and colors. Large bows with multiple loops and 12" or longer streamers are secured with cloth-covered wire (see pages 125–126 for bow-making instructions). Glue or sew ribbon to the bow backs for tying them to the pew posts or attach pew-bow hangers, available from most florists.

Fig. 8-8

Add special touches to pew bows, using one of the following ideas:

🍃 Tie on smaller bows of contrasting colors or wire other ribbons to the larger bow.

🍃 Tape or glue sprigs of baby's breath, fresh flowers, or silk floral sprays to the bows. (Fig. 8-9)

Fig. 8-9

🍃 Tie the bows with contrasting ribbon, either narrower or of another type, creating streamers from the ends.

🍃 Add fragrance to the bows, using drops of flower oil.

At more formal weddings, pew ribbons can be used in addition to the other pew decorations for reserving seats for family members or those you wish to honor. Ribbons or tulle yardage loosely draped across the ends of the pew will distinguish the reserved seats from those of the rest of the guests. The draping is then removed as the guests are seated or are ushered out.

Covered hearts

Add a romantic touch to any wedding or reception with simple heart-shaped decorations. (Fig. 8-10) They can hang from the pews, be attached to garlands, or used as table decorations.

Fig. 8-10

Wrap 6" to 8" *Styrofoam* hearts with satin ribbon in white or the wedding colors, gluing the ribbon ends to secure them. (See page 130 for gluing tips.) Make ribbon bows with streamers and glue them to the hearts. For additional decoration, add floral or beading sprays.

Wedding banners or flags

Herald in the wedding day with a decorative banner or flag. It can hang as a decoration for

the ceremony, point out the location of the reception, or enhance
the other reception decor. (Fig.
8-11) Paint, glue, sew, or iron
decorations to any type of banner.
As the base, use a plain purchased canvas banner or make
one from paper, lustrous bridal
fabric, stiff netting, felt, or a
water-repellent fabric.

Fig. 8-11

The banner size will depend
on its use and location, but make
certain the design is large enough
to be seen easily from a distance.
If the banner will become a keepsake and hang in the couple's new
home, make it an appropriate size
for a wall hanging. Use a wooden
dowel for hanging to prevent the
banner from drooping—a ⅜"
dowel for smaller banners or a ¾"
dowel for larger, heavier ones.

Make the dowel casing by turning
the top edge to the wrong side
and gluing, sewing, or fusing it in
place. Measure to make sure the
dowel slides through the casing
easily but is held snugly in place.
Hang the banner with clear fishline or thin picture wire.

Don't limit the banner's lower
edge to a straight design, but consider curving it, cutting "V"s, or
using any other shaping. (Fig. 8-
12) Finish the edges of ravelly
fabric banners by one of the following methods:

Fig. 8-12

🌺 Serge-finish with a short, narrow, balanced stitch for a tightly
woven fabric or a wider balanced
stitch for a loosely woven fabric.

🌺 Hem the edges by serge-finishing,
turning a narrow hem ¼" to the

wrong side, and top-stitching.
Or, without using a serger, turn a
double hem ¼" to the wrong side
and top-stitch.

🌺 Fuse a hem by pressing a precut ¾"-wide strip of paper-
backed fusible web on the wrong-
side edges. Then remove the
paper and press ⅜" to the wrong
side, fusing it in place.

🌺 Fringe one short end of a
loosely woven fabric, finishing the
other edges using one of the
methods above.

Another option is to make a
doubled banner by cutting it
twice the length desired plus ½"
for hem allowances. Press the
hem allowances to the wrong
side, fold the banner equally over
the dowel, and fuse or glue it in
place, enclosing the cut edges and
making the banner reversible.
On paper banners, glue pennies
as weights to the bottom, folding
and gluing a hem to the wrong
side to enclose them.

Trace, draw, or paint a design
on the banner, testing on small
scraps first. Embellishment possibilities include:

🌺 Attaching floral sprays, satin
roses, or paper flowers in a size
and number proportionate to the
banner size.

Cutting floral designs from printed fabric and gluing or fusing them to the banner. Outline the edges with glitter paints.

Gluing on padded satin hearts or lace motifs.

Attaching ball knobs to both ends of the dowel and painting both the knobs and dowel in a coordinating color.

Draping satin cording across the top of the banner, knotting it at the ends and leaving long streamers. (Fig. 8-13)

Tying ribbon bows at the corners with streamers extending.

Attaching decorative fringe, tassels, or beaded trim for added adornment.

Fig. 8-13

Planning the Reception Details

The reception can be as formal or as casual as you wish and may have a special theme. (See page 26 to review the planning details.)

Colorful balloons

Clusters of balloons tied with ribbons or a banner (see the previous suggestions) and coordinated with the wedding colors can mark the reception location.

> ### *Budget Helper*
>
> *Balloons are an economical and festive reception decoration, too, and can be a good alternative to elaborate floral arrangements.*

Balloons should be inflated with helium to keep them afloat. They can be festooned with rib-

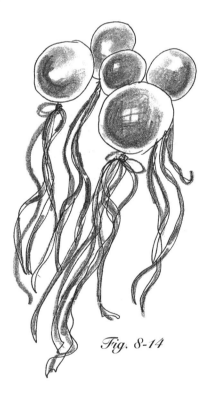

Fig. 8-14

bon streamers and the names of the couple can be printed on them. (Fig. 8-14) Have the balloons blown up the day of the wedding because they'll last only about eight hours.

Guest book and pen

There's no need to purchase an expensive guest registry set. Simply decorate a pen by wrapping on floral sprays, beading loops, and ribbon bows with white floral tape. Attach it to a pen holder with a white satin ribbon. (Fig. 8-15)

Fig. 8-15

Personalize a plain white guest book by wrapping wide beaded bridal lace or Battenberg lace around the front cover and gluing it on.

> **"** *My wedding was small and rather than have a guest book, my mother asked each guest to write or draw a message to us on a square of cotton fabric, using a permanent marker. She then embroidered over the messages and incorporated the squares into a quilt. The quilt has been a special treasure to us for over 20 years now.* **"**
>
> *Ceci Johnson*
> Quick & Easy Ways with Ribbon

Table coverings

The manner in which the food is displayed can mean the difference between an elegant buffet and a mediocre one. The table coverings can be multilayered to bring in the wedding colors, relate to a theme, or add a festive feeling. Consider using a bright print or floral fabric, a solid-colored plastic tablecloth in one of the wedding colors, or colored lamé yardage under a lace tablecloth or white netting. Just tuck any fabric raw ends under—there's no need to finish them. (Fig. 8-16)

Fig. 8-16

Another option is to cover each table with a white tablecloth and top it with crisscrossed runners of plain or printed fabric. You won't need to hem the runners—simply cut them with a rotary cutter and pink or scallop the edges.

> **"** *To save money and time, rent full-length tablecloths. Bonus: laundering is usually included. Then add accent colors with your own fabric, paper runners, and/or napkins.* **"**
>
> *Gail Brown*
> Quick Napkin Creations

For a draped effect, tie up the corners of the tablecloth overhang, pinning large bows of the wedding colors over the gathered areas. Or tie tulle yardage in swags around the table and pin the bows to it. (Fig. 8-17)

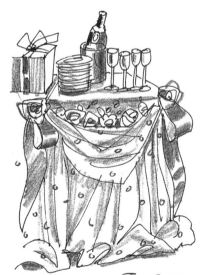

Fig. 8-17

Fig. 8-18

Table centerpieces

Use the table centerpieces to enhance the mood of the occasion. One inexpensive idea is to use mirror tiles as a centerpiece base to reflect the color and glitter of the other table decorations. (Fig. 8-18) The tiles come square, round, or in various other shapes. For an added touch, glue 1½"- to 2"-wide gathered lace around each tile. Crocheted or lace doilies can also be used over a colored tablecloth as a base for small arrangements. Use small floral arrangements, votive candles with ribbon bows, floral sprays, and/or wire-edged ribbons or cording draped around the arrangements to complete a festive centerpiece. Glue pearl beading to the top rim of a votive candle for another elegant touch. (Fig. 8-19)

Fig. 8-19

Add color to a candle holder or bud vase by wrapping fabric around the base. Use fabric scraps left over from the bridesmaid dresses or wedding gown and add a layer of tulle over it:

1. Cut a square of fabric and tulle using pinking shears or a rotary cutter with a pinking blade.

2. Wrap the fabric and tulle loosely around the base of the candle holder or vase, securing it with a colored rubber band matching the fabric. Tie several strands of ⅛"-wide satin ribbon over the rubber band. (Fig. 8-20)

Fig. 8-20

> **"**Inexpensively turn rented table cloths into outstanding reception decor by laying natural foliage (I used myrtle) down the center of each table for a sit-down dinner. Every foot or two, alternate country crock pots filled with wet sand and wholesale flowers with short drinking glasses filled with water, salad oil, and floating candle disks. The floating candles even work well out of doors and provide enough soft light for a romantic atmosphere. Write the couple's names and the date on the crocks, using a permanent marker, and give them away at the end to everyone who helped.**"**
>
> *Nancy Ward*
> Stamping Made Easy

Festive Food

Food is the highlight of the reception and probably the largest expense in the wedding budget. The cost will vary with the type of food served.

Budget Helper

See page 26 for suggestions on selecting a caterer and other considerations for organizing the reception.

Food service choices include a buffet (the least expensive), a semibuffet, or plate service. The furniture needed will also depend on the type of service. For example, for buffet service, it isn't necessary to have tables and chairs for each guest, but do have some for the older people attending. Most reception sites will have tables and chairs available, but if you're holding a reception at home or outdoors, you will need to rent or borrow them. Tables in various shapes, chairs, dishes, and glassware are all available from party rental services. Ask whether delivery and pickup are offered.

Budget Helper

When renting party supplies or furniture, be sure to check how long the rental period is and when you will have to return the items to avoid paying extra.

Sanity Saver

When organizing your own reception, eliminate stress by enlisting different family members or friends to oversee the food service and act as a general host or hostess of the event. For both positions, you'll need a person who stays cool under pressure.

There also needs to be a person in charge of several other crucial areas: kitchen, buffet, beverages, and cleanup. If friends prepare and serve the food, they should label the dishes to avoid confusion later and place appropriate serving utensils with each plate or bowl.

When planning a menu, keep it simple, offering only four or five foods. Vary the colors, sizes, and shapes of the foods chosen. To select appropriate items, control the costs, and plan the amount of food and the serving sizes needed, follow these guidelines:

Place the inexpensive bulky foods, such as pasta, salad, and rolls, first on the serving tables.

If serving a salad, avoid greens because they can be more difficult to eat while standing.

Plan any hors d'oeuvres to serve four per person per hour. Serve 3 ounces of meat per person and 1½ ounces of salad.

Estimate two to three drinks per adult for the first hour and fewer after that. Children will drink more (nonalcoholic, of course).

Use 4- or 5-ounce glasses for wine or champagne and 8-ounce cups for punch and coffee.

Select a light punch for a hot summer wedding—a punch with sherbet or ice cream is not thirst-quenching. (See page 49 for appropriate punch suggestions.)

Serve champagne or sparkling cider for the toast and the cutting of the cake only.

The wedding cake

The cake is often the focus of both the reception decorations and the food. (Fig. 8-21) It is usually multilayered and, traditionally, the top layer is taken home and frozen for the couple to enjoy on their first anniversary. The cake is often placed on a table of its own with the bridal bouquet on the table as a decoration. For added embellishment, drape netting, lace, or satin fabric on the table under the cake.

Fig. 8-21

Prices, quality, and tastes vary widely when selecting a wedding cake. Consider these options for staying within or cutting the budget (even drastically) and still having a cake to remember:

Buy from a local grocery store or supermarket bakery.

Purchase one small decorated layer cake and serve decorated sheet cakes.

Decorate a dummy cake and serve decorated sheet cakes. The dummy cake can be made from *Styrofoam* forms or various sizes of bandboxes, frosted and decorated as desired.

Frost and decorate a dummy upper layer, which is not to be cut.

Decorate a simple cake with flowers or floral sprays, either fresh or silk.

Budget Helper

Any cake topper used will add to the cost of the cake. Various cake tops in all price ranges can be found in gift, craft, and other stores. Flowers may be used with, or in place of, a cake top or to decorate the entire cake.

When decorating the cake with flowers, make sure they are of a nonpoisonous variety. Use fresh flowers and greenery on the top of the cake, cascading down the side, or around the bottom. Add the flowers just before the guests arrive for the ultimate fresh appearance. Various fresh-flower containers are used in cake decorating and are available from a florist or craft stores.

Ceremonial accessories

A decorated cake knife or server and toasting goblets will add to the festivities. Either use the tie-on decorations from a shower (see page 46), or a floral spray, ribbon roses, or another embellishment tied to the glasses or knife with ⅛"-wide satin ribbon. Or simply tie lightweight wire-edged ribbon or bendable ribbon into bows around the knife and goblets. (Fig. 8-22) See page 129 for detailed embellishment suggestions.

Fig. 8-22

Ornamental Champagne Wrapper

If you're serving champagne, wrap the bottles with an elegant covering. (Fig. 8-23)

Fig. 8-23

MATERIALS NEEDED FOR TWO WRAPPERS

An embroidered, monogrammed, or other decorated white linen napkin, approximately 12" square

Approximately 2⅓ yards of ½"- to ¾"-wide gathered lace

How-Tos

1. Cut the napkin in half diagonally, being sure the most elaborately decorated corners remain intact.

2. Fuse, glue, or sew a narrow hem on the cut edges.

3. Apply the lace to all the outside edges of the wrap by lapping the napkin over the lace straight edge and gluing, fusing, or sewing them together.

4. Tie the narrowed points around the necks of the champagne bottles.

Favors

By handing out favors at the reception, the bride and groom say thank you and give something back to those who came to celebrate and share in their joy. When planning the type of favors you'll use, keep in mind the number of guests—each person should receive one. Traditional favors include candies, Jordan almonds, or flowers enclosed in some type of wrapping. (Fig. 8-24)

Fig. 8-24

Favors are usually offered in some type of decorated container, such as a basket or bowl, and are handed out during the reception by the flower girl or other youngsters. The favors and their containers can also serve as table decorations, with the guests helping themselves. See pages 52 and 100 for ideas on decorating baskets to hold the favors.

Some less conventional favor ideas include:

🌿 A wedding poem printed on rice paper or parchment paper, rolled into a scroll and tied with raffia or a ribbon.

🌿 Packets of flower seeds.

🌿 Incense or candy wrapped in colored tissue paper and tied with a ribbon.

🌿 Decorated cookies in the shapes of bells and hearts.

🌿 Small straw hats purchased at a craft store. Glue on a floral spray, ribbon bows, and streamers in the wedding colors.

🌿 Single flowers with the date or the names of the bride and groom printed on ribbon ties (or simply tie the flowers with a coordinating color tulle or ribbon bow). (Fig. 8-25)

Fig. 8-25

🌿 Circles of white or another color tulle gathered up around candies, nuts, or birdseed and tied with a coordinating color of ribbon or satin cording. After tying, fluff out the tulle on top.

🌿 Miniature champagne glasses purchased from a craft store, filled with candies or birdseed wrapped with the tulle and ribbon as described above.

🌿 Wrapped soaps, potpourri, or herbs.

🌿 Tiny lace bags filled with candies, nuts, or birdseed.

> **"**My daughter was married in England, where they have a charming custom of serving frosted square fruit cake as the wedding cake. Since it is preserved, slices can be sent to absent friends and relatives to let them be a part of the wedding. The frosting is quite elaborate and looks like lace, roses, and ribbons.**"**
>
> *Robbie Fanning*
> The Complete Book of
> Machine Quilting

Little Lace Favor Bags

Quickly make pretty small bags to hold the favors of your choice. (Fig. 8-26)

Fig. 8-26

MATERIALS NEEDED

One yard of 45"-wide lace fabric (will make 108 bags) or 6" of 2½"-wide lace ribbon (for each bag)

One yard of 45"-wide tulle

54 yards of ⅛"- or ¼"-wide satin ribbon in the wedding colors (for 108 bags)—each bag uses ½ yard of ribbon

Pinking shears or a rotary cutter with a pinking or scalloping blade plus a cutting mat

Birdseed, foil-covered candy, or Jordan almonds

CUTTING DIRECTIONS

Place the tulle on the wrong side of the lace yardage and cut 2½" by 6" strips through both layers using the pinking shears or rotary cutter. Or cut the lace ribbon into 6" lengths and cut the tulle separately.

Cut the satin ribbon into 18" lengths, one for each bag.

Fig. 8-27

HOW-TOS

1. With the tulle strip on the wrong side of the lace, fold the fabric in half lengthwise, wrong sides together, and stitch a narrow seam on both sides. (Fig. 8-27)

2. Fill each bag half full of birdseed, candy, or almonds and tie it closed with a ribbon.

CHAPTER NINE
Moments to Remember

In all the excitement of the occasion, don't forget to plan for the future. There are several things you can do to preserve the fond memories of your special day.

> *"Many copy shops can create personalized, color calendars from photographs. For the couple's first Christmas, choose twelve funny or informal photographs from the wedding preparations and wedding and surprise them with a calendar of remembrances."*
>
> *Ceci Johnson*
> Quick & Easy Ways with Ribbon

Heirlooming the Gown

You may decide to keep the wedding gown as an heirloom for a loved one's wedding in the future, take it apart to remake into mementos, or alter it to wear later. In any event, ask the bridal salon for recommendations on a good dry cleaner.

Budget Helper

Shop around for a dry cleaner because prices can vary. Some cleaners may refuse to clean a wedding dress, especially if beads are glued on rather than sewn. The minimum price a reputable cleaner will charge for heirlooming a wedding dress is $40.

Wait to dry-clean the dress until several weeks after the wedding. Some stains do not appear immediately, so waiting allows time for the dry cleaner to see

and treat them appropriately. Be sure to tell the dry cleaner about anything you know may have been spilled on the dress. Do plan to treat the gown within a month after the wedding, however, because the longer the stains remain, the harder they are to remove. Even perspiration stains can destroy the fabric.

To preserve the gown, store it (after cleaning) in acid-free tissue paper and roll tissue "pillows" into the sleeves and bodice to prevent permanent wrinkles. Do not store it in plastic, but instead loosely wrap it in unbleached prewashed cotton or muslin or place it in a large, unsealed box wrapped in a cotton bag. Or use a specially designed bag now on the market to help keep air away from the dress fabric to prevent its deterioration.

Another storage option is to hang the gown, which will allow it to age evenly. Consider making

a cotton garment bag out of pre-washed muslin or a sheet. Hang the dress on a padded hanger and measure its length and width. Make the bag large enough to generously cover the dress without crushing it, adding extra length for gathering up and tying the top closed around the hanger. (Fig. 9-1)

Fig. 9-1

Store the gown in a cool dry place. After a year, you may want to take it out again and check for stains before rewrapping it. Don't store your dress on a humid day because the moisture trapped inside may cause mildew and ruin it.

If you're planning to wear the dress for other occasions later, select it with that in mind. A simple, unembellished dress may be shortened and a scarf or colorful belt or sash can be added to change the look. On a more elaborate gown, you may also need to remove the train and beading as well as altering some areas, such as the sleeves.

If you're certain the dress won't be worn in the future, you may want to use parts of it as remembrances. Make or trim lingerie or an elegant robe. Sew a bassinet skirt to pass on lovingly to a child. Or construct other mementos such as those featured later in this chapter.

Preserving the Flowers

Another fun way to savor your wedding memories is to dry flowers from the wedding and showers and use them later as lasting reminders. Try one of the several methods below.

Drying

Dry the flowers by spreading them out on flat trays or cookie sheets. Take the bouquet apart so that air can circulate around each flower. Put them in a 200-degree oven overnight until they are papery to the touch.

Make a pretty wall hanging by gluing some of the dried flowers to a grapevine wreath base, adding ribbons and bows. (See the gluing tips on page 130.) Or spray-paint a straw wreath form white or natural and glue on the flowers and bows. Attach a wire loop for hanging. (Fig. 9-2)

To preserve a bouquet intact, first remove all of the foliage. Re-tie the flowers at the end of the stems with cotton string. Place the bouquet upside down in a brown paper bag and keep it in a dry place for three to four weeks.

Fig. 9-2

Hasten the drying process by using a microwave oven. Dry only the flowers that are in good shape. Discard any that are wilted or fully opened. This method preserves the natural color. Trim the stems close to the blossoms and dip the flowers into silica gel to add moisture and yet allow them to keep their shape. Cover the flowers with the gel and put them in a microwave for a short time (following manufacturer's instructions) until the gel is heated. Then remove them and allow them to dry for at least 12 more hours.

You can also preserve the flowers by spraying them with hair-spray. Wire the blossoms together and wrap the stems with floral tape. Arrange the dried flowers with a large bow in the center and use them as a wall decoration. (Fig. 9-3)

Fig. 9-3

Pressing

Pressed flowers can be used as a pretty decorative accent on stationery, in a framed memento box, or for other craft projects. Single flat flowers are the easiest ones to press. Remove the stems close to the blossom base. For flowers that aren't flat and have multiple layers of petals, remove the petals and press them separately.

Handle the flowers as little as possible, placing them on blotting paper or a folded paper towel. Cover them with another sheet of paper and sandwich the layers between stiff pieces of cardboard. Place them in a warm room with large books on top or use a flower press for five to six weeks until the flowers are dry.

Use the pressed flowers to make charming thank-you notes. Purchase the note cards or make them from parchment or recycled paper. Glue a pressed flower to the front of each card as an

Fig. 9-4

embellishment and hand-print the couple's names or "thank you" next to it. (Fig. 9-4)

Floral potpourri

To make potpourri from the wedding flowers, remove the petals and scatter them in a flat basket or on a cookie sheet. Cover them with a piece of cheesecloth to protect against dust and set them out of the way until they're dry.

Carefully mix the potpourri in a large bowl, adding lemon oil, bath oil, or herbs such as lavender to the dried petals. An option is to mix spices, such as cinnamon or cloves. Sprinkle the mixture with salt and place it in a jar for six weeks, shaking periodically to blend. Wrap the potpourri in several layers of tulle, tied with ribbon from the bridal bouquet. Or enclose it in a lace bag made from sections of the wedding gown (see page 120).

Caring for the Gifts

If your first home is small, you may not have room to display all of the valuable crystal, china, or collectibles you received as wedding gifts. And depending on your lifestyle, you may not have the occasion to use them. To prevent breaking or chipping, keep each item in the original box or packaging. If you do display the gifts, place them high up out of the way to prevent accidental breakage.

Other Remembrances

There are many simple projects you can make to preserve the happy memories of the wedding. Use the same fabrics, laces, and colors as the bride and her attendants.

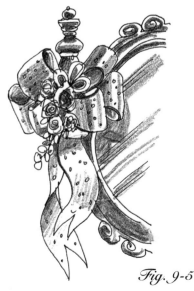

Fig. 9-5

Budget Helper

Convert pew bows to door-handle hangers or use them to decorate a dresser mirror. (Fig. 9-5)

Fragrant Memories Sachet

Keep a drawer or closet sweetly scented with potpourri sealed in a lovely lace bag. (Fig. 9-6)

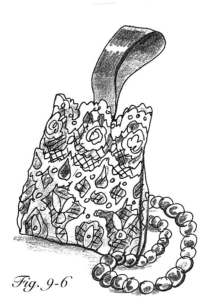

Fig. 9-6

MATERIALS NEEDED

One rectangle (approximately 9" by 3") of embroidered lace with a motif that can be trimmed (the exact size will depend on the lace motif)

8" of ½"-wide satin ribbon

Potpourri (purchase or follow the previous instructions)

HOW-TOS

1. Trim the lace motif at both short ends to form attractive finished edges.

2. Fold the rectangle crosswise, right sides together, and sew or serge ¼" seams on both long edges.

3. Turn the bag right side out and fill it three-quarters full with potpourri.

4. To form the loop, fold the ribbon in half and pin the ends 1¼" inside the bag, centered on the upper edge.

5. Sew across the bag top 1" from the upper edge, catching the ribbon ends in the stitching. Slip the loop over a hanger or use the sachet in a dresser drawer.

Embellished Photo Album

Personalize an album cover as a remembrance of that special day, using the fabric and trim of your choice. (Fig. 9-7)

Fig. 9-7

MATERIALS NEEDED

One photo album

One piece of polyester batting the exact size of the entire outer cover of the album

Satin or taffeta fabric, (see Cutting Directions)

Matching batiste, poly-cotton, or polyester lining fabric, equal to the cover fabric

Embroidered lace, equal to the cover fabric

Pearl beading equal to the entire circumference of the cover

One yard of ⅝"-wide satin ribbon

A glue gun or quick-drying craft glue

CUTTING DIRECTIONS

Measure the outer cover of the closed album from the front around to the back. Draw a pattern equal to that size, adding on enough extra on both sides to wrap around on the inside of both album covers to within 2" of the center of the spine. (Fig. 9-8) Add ⅜" seam allowances on all sides.

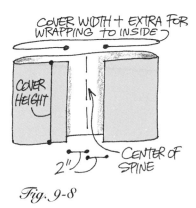

Fig. 9-8

Using the pattern, cut one piece each of the cover fabric, lining, and lace.

HOW-TOS

Sew or serge all seams using ¼" allowances.

1. With the album closed, glue the batting to the outside of the cover.

2. Sandwich the lace between the satin and the lining with the lace wrong side against the satin right side and the lace right side against the lining right side. Seam all four edges, leaving an opening for turning.

3. Trim the corners and turn the fabric right side out with the lining on one side and the

lace on the other. Hand-sew the opening closed and press carefully.

4. Fold the short ends of the cover, lining sides together, toward the center, leaving a 4" space between the edges.

5. Edge-stitch the upper and lower edges together. (Fig. 9-9)

6. Open the album and slip the cover onto it.

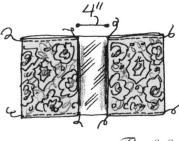

Fig. 9-9

7. Cut the ribbon into two equal lengths and glue one end of each piece at the center of the front and back outer edges.

8. Beginning at the center of the lower edge, glue the beading around the album's outer edges, covering the ribbon ends. Tie the album closed with a bow.

Optional: Eliminate the ribbon ties. Instead, finish a strip of coordinating fabric and glue it around the album, tying a larger bow on the top. (Fig. 9-10)

Fig. 9-10

Quilted Wedding Sampler

Create a special sampler featuring treasured mementos of the wedding day. (Fig. 9-11)

Fig. 9-11

MATERIALS NEEDED

Scraps of satin, ribbons, lace yardage, and other fabrics from the wedding dress (or fabrics of a similar appearance)

One 16" by 19" rectangle of matching satin

One 16" by 19" rectangle of batting

Dried flowers (see the instructions beginning on page 118), lace motifs, beading, bows, lace trim, and any other meaningful decoration

How-Tos

Sew or serge all seams using ¼" allowances.

1. Piece the fabric and ribbon scraps together to a size larger than 16" by 19". Cut a 16" by 19" rectangle from the pieced material for the sampler background.

2. Place the solid satin rectangle and the pieced sampler right sides together. Layer the batting underneath with the satin on top. Seam all four edges, leaving an opening for turning. Trim all four corners and turn the sampler right side out. Hand-sew the opening closed.

3. Quilt all of the piecing seams through all layers.

4. To finish the sampler, top-stitch beading to some of the seamlines, using a long, narrow zigzag. Top-stitch lace trim around the outer edges. Randomly attach dried flowers, lace motifs, and other desired trim.

Framed Souvenir Invitation

Display a copy of the wedding invitation in an attractive frame, adding dried wedding flowers and a bow for embellishment. (Fig. 9-12)

Fig. 9-12

MATERIALS NEEDED

One picture frame, large enough to frame the invitation

White spray paint

A wedding invitation

Fabric from the wedding gown or bridesmaid dresses

Dried flowers and ribbon from the wedding

Pearl beading equal to the inside-edge measurement of the frame

A glue gun

How-Tos

1. Spray the frame white.

2. Cover the inside of the frame with the dress fabric and glue it in place.

3. Center the invitation in the middle of the frame and glue it to the fabric.

4. Insert the fabric and invitation into the frame.

5. Glue a spray of dried flowers to the frame's upper corner, adding a bow and streamers.

6. Glue beading around the inside edge of the frame.

Fond Remembrances Video Box

Store the videotaped memories of a wonderful wedding in a pretty decorated box. You'll always be able to locate it quickly. (Fig. 9-13)

Fig. 9-13

MATERIALS NEEDED

One white plastic video case

Polyester batting the exact size of the outer cover of the case when closed

Satin or polyester fabric the exact size of the case cover plus 1" extra in both length and width

1½ yards of 1"-wide satin ribbon in a wedding color

A glue gun

HOW-TOS

1. Glue the batting to the outside of the case, making certain the lid will close.

2. With the case open and the batting side down, center the case over the wrong side of the fabric. Fold the fabric over the inside lip of the case and glue it in place. Trim the excess fabric.

3. Glue the ribbon around the case frame, covering the plastic.

4. Center and glue ribbon horizontally around the entire case cover and vertically on the lid, wrapping the edges to the inside of the lips.

5. Tie the remaining ribbon into a bow and glue it to the lid where the ribbons cross.

Optional: If the case will be stacked on a shelf with other videos, eliminate the ribbon and bow and monogram the cover before gluing it to the case. (Fig. 9-14)

Fig. 9-14

Victorian Lace Keepsake Cases

Make a dainty case from wedding fabric and lace to hold keepsake letters, lingerie, or hosiery. (Fig. 9-15)

Fig. 9-15

MATERIALS NEEDED

One 10" by 18" rectangle of wedding fabric

One 10" by 18" rectangle of embroidered lace

One 10" by 18" rectangle of batiste or poly-cotton for lining

One 10" by 18" rectangle of fusible fleece

Optional: ⅞ yard of 1½"-wide double-faced satin ribbon (for a tie)

Ribbon, braid, lace trim, flowers, and/or bows (for embellishment)

HOW-TOS

1. Fuse the fleece to the wrong side of the lining rectangle.

2. Sandwich the lace between the lining and the fabric, placing it right sides together with the lining and wrong sides together with the fabric right side. Sew or serge all four edges using ¼" seam allowances and leaving an opening for turning.
   Optional: To add a tie, cut the ribbon into two equal lengths. Center one cut edge of each on the short ends of the rectangle, between the lace and the lining. Be careful not to catch the loose ends in the seaming, then trim them diagonally after step 3.

3. Turn the rectangle right side out, with the lace on one side and the lining on the other. Hand-sew the opening closed.

4. Fold the rectangle in half crosswise with the lining sides together. Edge-stitch along both sides, seaming them together to form the case.

5. Hand-sew ribbon, braid, flowers, or bows onto the case to embellish it.

APPENDIX

Beautiful Bows

Basic Decorator Bow

Ribbons and bows, either simple or elaborate, are usually a part of the wedding decorations and embellishments. Available at all sewing and craft stores, ribbons come in a wide variety of types and widths. In addition to simple and elegant satin ribbons with smooth edges, you'll find many novelty ribbons, including those trimmed with decorative picot edges, stiffened with wire edges for easy shaping, and even a special bendable ribbon in which the entire ribbon surface is flexible and retains its shape.

Any ribbon can be shaped into a wide assortment of bows to use during the wedding festivities. Use florist wire, wire cutters, pliers, and utility scissors when making bows. Here are a few of the simplest and most used types.

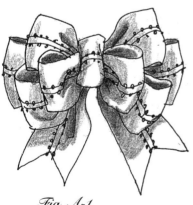

Fig. A-1

1. For a bow approximately 8" across, use 3 yards of ribbon (Fig. A-1). Measure a tail of about 14" and squeeze the ribbon together at that point. (Fig. A-2)

8" OF RIBBON MAKES 4" LOOP.

Fig. A-2

2. Make a loop on one side using 8" to 9" of ribbon with the right side out, twist the ribbon in the center, and repeat for the opposite side.

3. Continuing to hold the bow in the center, make slightly smaller loops on top of the first ones, until you have four

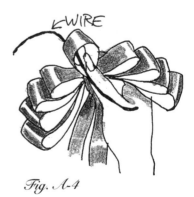

Fig. A-3

on each side. (Fig. A-3) Be sure to continue twisting so that the right side of the ribbon is always to the outside.

4. Finish the bow by making a center loop, thread a wire through it, and twist tightly to secure the center. (Fig. A-4)

WIRE

Fig. A-4

5. Adjust the loops attractively on both sides and trim the tails diagonally or into inverted "V"s.

Larger Bow

For an oversized version of the basic bow (Fig. A-5), used for pew bows and with larger floral decorations, try this simple option with an extra set of tails:

Fig. A-5

1. For a bow approximately 12" across, use 8 yards of wide ribbon. Follow the instructions above, making extra loops, if desired, to fill out the bow.

2. Before wiring the bow together, add one or more sets of long tails. (Fig. A-6)

Fig. A-6

Note: If the ribbon is thick and heavy, you may want to double the wire for extra strength.

Combination Bow

For a more elaborate effect, use two ribbons together when making a basic bow. Layering a lace ribbon over a wider satin one gives an elegant effect. (Fig. A-7) Remember to twist both layers together as you form the loops, centering the top ribbon and keeping it taut against the other layer.

Fig. A-7

Ribbon Rosettes

Super-Simple Folded Rosettes

One of the most popular decorative notions for wedding embellishment, rosettes can be purchased ready-made at fabric and craft stores. But to save money or to get a perfect color match, you easily can make them yourself. If you can't find the ribbon you want, make it by serge-finishing or hemming the edges of fabric strips.

A few folds and a gentle pull are all you need to form these pretty rosettes (Fig. A-8):

1. Using 3/8"-wide or wider ribbon, cut a piece approximately 20" long for each rosette. (Narrower ribbon is more difficult to work with.)

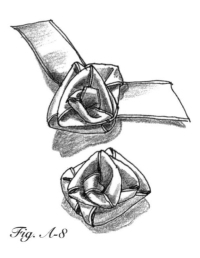

Fig. A-8

2. Fold the center of the ribbon diagonally so that the tails form a right angle, then continue folding the tails under alternately, one at a time, until you reach the ends. (Fig. A-9) You will make about 20 folds. To hold the folded ribbon together securely, keep your thumb on top and your fingers underneath as you work.

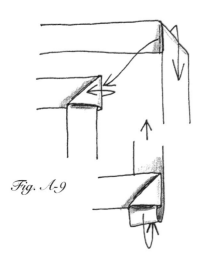

Fig. A-9

3. At the last fold, use your thumb and forefinger to hold the two ribbon ends together. Turn the rosette over and allow the folds to fan out like an accordion. (Fig. A-10)

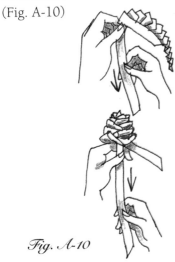

Fig. A-10

4. Gently pull the bottom ribbon tail to form the flower. Place a straight pin through the center of the rosette to hold it in place until you hand-stitch the bottom layers together. Either cut off the ribbon tails or let them extend out decoratively from under the rosette after it is attached to the project.

Rolled Rosettes

Make any rose shape, from a bud to a full bloom, by rolling a length of ribbon while folding it at the same time (Fig. A-11):

1. To begin, fold the ribbon diagonally, a few inches from one end, so that the tails form a right angle.

2. Roll one outer edge over the ribbon right side several times to form a tight center, then fold the other tail diagonally again to the underside and begin wrapping it around the center. (Fig. A-12) Hold the bottom of the bud firmly as you wrap.

Fig. A-11

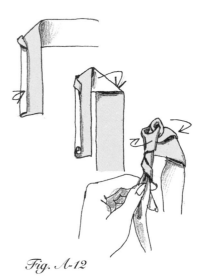

Fig. A-12

3. Continue rolling to the end of the folded section, folding again to the underside, and rolling again, flaring the top of the ribbon as you work. You will see the flower begin to develop.

4. When the rosette reaches the size you want, wrap the remaining ribbon down around the beginning tail, continuing to hold on to the bottom of the flower. Then wrap florist wire securely around the base of the rosette and down around the tails. (Fig. A-13) If the stem will be visible, cover the ribbon and wire with floral tape, wrapping in leaves as you go.

Fig. A-13

Gathered Rosettes

Another rosette variation, usually one that is fuller and more showy, can be made with gathering or shirring. (Fig. A-14) See pages 84-85 for a simple bud variation of a gathered rosette.

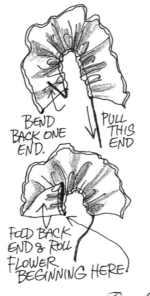

BEND BACK ONE END. PULL THIS END

FOLD BACK END & ROLL FLOWER BEGINNING HERE!

Fig. A-15

Fig. A-17

Fig. A-14

For the simplest gathered rosette, use a 12" to 15" length of wire-edged ribbon:

1. Gather up the ribbon over the wire on one long edge, folding back the wire on one end to keep it from pulling out. (Fig. A-15)

2. Fold the beginning raw end at a right angle toward the gathered edge and start rolling the gathered edge to form a flower shape. Make the rosette as tight or full as you wish.

3. Use the wire tail at the opposite end to wrap and secure the bottom of the rosette. (Fig. A-16)

Fig. A-16

Optional: Use a decorative center stamen for a more elaborate rosette and gather the fabric around it. (Fig. A-17) A stamen

can also be used for a variation of the rolled rosettes mentioned above.

When making a gathered rosette without wire-edged ribbon, gather one long edge using a sewing machine or serger. Then form the flower following the instructions above. For an elegant satin rosette, fold a ribbon or fabric strip lengthwise so that the fold forms the petals and the loose edges are gathered together.

FOLD

BOTH EDGES GATHERED

Fig. A-18

Other Decorative Touches

In addition to bows and rosettes, you'll find many other attractive embellishments at craft- and floral-supply stores and sewing stores. In larger metropolitan areas, there even may be discount outlets where you can shop.

Your project can be as simple or as elaborately embellished as you want it to be. Here are a few of the easy-to-use notions you should be able to locate without much trouble and at a minimal price:

Narrow satin ribbon—Either with plain or picot edges, narrow ribbon streamers and additional simple bows can add color to your project and create a more elaborate embellishment. (Fig. A-19)

Lace ribbon—Available in a variety of widths, lace ribbon streamers and wrappings can add a delicate touch.

Floral sprays and garlands—Even if you choose to use all fresh flowers for the bouquets and arrangements, silk floral sprays can add a lovely embellishment to other decorations and projects as well.

Decorative doves, hearts, and other appropriate notions—Sometimes a project or decoration will need just that special touch. Look for wedding-oriented accessories at surprisingly low costs. (Fig. A-20)

Fig. A-21

stores to further embellish your rosettes or less elaborate floral sprays. (Fig. A-21)

Pearl bead strands and sprays—By far the most common beading used for weddings, pearls are attractive as part of floral sprays and garlands, used as loops and streamers with ribbon accents, or as an added decorative effect. (Fig. A-22)

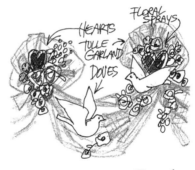

Fig. A-20

Tulle or illusion—Often used for veils (see page ___), these filmy fabrics can also be used for garlands, large bows, and other accents. They're especially attractive when combined with ribbons, beads, floral sprays, and other decorative notions.

Floral leaves in silver, gold, or green—Use silk or metallic leaves from floral- or craft-supply

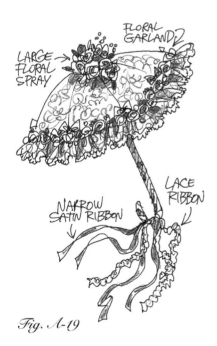

Fig. A-19

Fig. A-22

Bridal appliqués—A wide variety of intricate ready-made appliqués are available for embellishing everything from the wedding gown and accessories to projects and keepsakes. You'll find a large price range, too, so shop around for the less expensive ones when the quality will not be as important in the finished item.

Depending on the specific project you are making, you may choose to attach the decorative touches by quickly wrapping, tying, or wiring them on. Other options include sewing or gluing the embellishments in position.

Glue Gun Techniques

On many projects where you want to attach embellishments permanently, a glue gun can be the quickest and easiest answer. Originally available only as "hot glue guns," technology has advanced to include "low-temp" guns as well. These handy tools melt sticks of specially formulated glue and release a fine glue line when you squeeze the trigger.

The hot glue guns provide more holding power, give you a longer working time, and are good when you are working on large areas at once. The lower-temperature models are good for smaller jobs and are less apt to cause burned fingers. This advantage is especially good for delicate materials or when youngsters are using the glue gun.

In addition to the different temperatures available, glue guns come in a variety of types. Mini guns, small and often inexpensively priced, are adequate for small projects and detail work. Midsize and larger guns are better for big jobs.

Glue sticks used in glue guns vary with the kind of gun, so follow the manufacturer's recommendation. In addition to all-purpose glue sticks, versions now come especially formulated for fabric or wood and others are colored or have glitter added.

Follow these easy tips for success in any of your glue gun projects:

🖎 Carefully read the instructions for your brand and model before using your glue gun.

🖎 Protect your work surface with a specially designed glue pad or disposable paper before beginning the project.

🖎 When it's hot but not in use, rest the gun on a stand or on an old plate or other heat-resistant glass dish.

🖎 If the gun has its own attached wire stand, use the edge of the work surface to press it in or back out as you work.

🖎 Work slowly and methodically to avoid excess drips and glue strings.

🖎 You will have *some* wispy glue strings with all gun and glue-stick types—sometimes more than others. To minimize the strings, let up on the trigger before pulling the gun away from the project. Then let the strings that do form dry where they land and just pull them away when dry. Trying to fight them when they're wet is much more difficult.

🖎 To keep the gun nozzle clean during your project, have a box of tissues or a paper towel handy and wipe off any excess before you set the gun down each time.

🖎 To avoid burns, especially with a hot-type gun, apply lotion liberally to your hands before beginning a project. If you will be using one finger to position beads or other small items, wrap it with adhesive tape or a *Band-Aid* first. Another option for applying small items is to use surgical tweezers and keep your fingers out of the glue.

🖎 When applying a large, heavy item, hold it in place for at least one minute to allow the glue to set. Or wire it on first and reinforce the wiring with glue. Begin with the largest embellishment first and add other smaller ones after each previous one is in place.

🖎 When you are finished using the glue gun, simply turn it off. Don't try to pull the leftover glue stick out. When you turn on the gun again, it will remelt and use the glue that is left in it.

Index

Naomi Baker is a nationally recognized sewing and serging authority who writes regularly for major industry publications and has co-authored nine previous Chilton books with Tammy Young. She specializes in technique research and development and is well known for her sewing and crafting skills.

Reared in the Midwest, Naomi is a clothing and textiles graduate of Iowa State University and worked as an extension agent for five years. After working an additional ten years for Stretch & Sew, and experimenting with virtually every home serger on the market at that time, she decided to begin her own sewing consulting business.

In addition to her writing, Naomi is a consulting editor for the *Serger Update* newsletter, makes frequent guest appearances on national television shows, and teaches at special workshops and conventions across the country. She is also involved in numerous volunteer activities in her community.

Naomi lives and works in Springfield, Oregon, with her husband, family, and a house full of fabric, sewing supplies, and state-of-the-art equipment. In the past, she's helped plan and sew for numerous weddings, but this book took on special significance as she simultaneously assisted with the first marriage among her own three children.

Tammy Young is known for her creative ideas and techniques and for giving precise, detailed instructions. A prolific writer, she has co-authored twelve previous Chilton books and continues to write for the *Sewing Update* and *Serger Update* newsletters, which she founded and managed until selling them in 1991.

She is also a sewing-industry consultant to Chilton and edits the *Sewing & Crafts Merchandiser* newsletter, which the company sends quarterly to independent retailers. And as a freelancer, she writes press releases for a San Francisco public relations firm.

Tammy grew up in Oregon and has a home economics degree from Oregon State University. She has an extensive background in the ready-to-wear fashion industry, having worked for major companies including Pendleton Woolen Mills, Jantzen, and Lily of France. She was also an extension agent and a high school home economics teacher.

Living and working in the heart of San Francisco, Tammy enjoys tackling a wide variety of creative projects and dreaming up ideas to try in her "spare time." She's now hard at work on a guide to glue crafting, to be published by Chilton in 1995.